# Summary

# The Green Thumb Guide: Cultivating Bounty

## Planting, Nurturing, and Harvesting: A Comprehensive Manual for Growing and Preserving Your Own Vegetables

**Rowan Fletcher**

# Chapter 1: The Basics of Vegetable Gardening

Welcome to the wonderful world of vegetable gardening, where you can grow your own fresh, healthy produce right in your own backyard. Whether you have a vast expanse of land or a small balcony, gardening offers numerous benefits, including the satisfaction of growing your own food and connecting with nature. This chapter will serve as your guide, taking you through the basics of vegetable gardening, from selecting the right location to harvesting your bountiful produce.

## 1.1 Selecting the Perfect Spot

Before you start digging and planting, it's essential to choose the ideal location for your vegetable garden. Factors such as sunlight, soil quality, and accessibility should be considered.

Sunlight is vital for the growth and overall productivity of your vegetable plants. Look for an area in your yard that receives at least 6-8 hours of direct sunlight per day. Vegetables like tomatoes, peppers, and cucumbers require ample sunshine to thrive.

Next, evaluate the quality of your soil. Most vegetables prefer well-draining soil rich in organic matter. Conduct a soil test to determine the pH level and nutrient content of your soil. You can purchase at-home soil testing kits or consult your local agricultural extension office for professional assistance.

Accessibility is another key factor to consider. Ensure that your vegetable garden is easily accessible for watering, weeding, and harvesting. Having a water source nearby is particularly important to provide consistent moisture to your plants.

## 1.2 Preparing the Soil

Once you have selected the perfect spot, it's time to prepare the soil for your vegetable garden. Start by clearing away any debris, rocks, or weeds that may hinder plant growth. If you have heavy clay soil, consider loosening it up by incorporating organic matter such as compost, aged manure, or peat moss. This will improve drainage and provide essential nutrients to your plants.

Afterward, use a garden fork or spade to turn over the soil, breaking up any clumps and creating a loose, crumbly texture. Remove any persistent weeds by hand or use a garden hoe to cut them at the roots and prevent competition with your vegetables.

## 1.3 Choosing the Right Vegetables

Now comes the exciting part – choosing the vegetables you want to grow in your garden. Consider your family's preferences, climate, and available space when making your selection. Some popular vegetables for beginners include tomatoes, lettuce, carrots, radishes, and beans.

When deciding which varieties to plant, consider your climate zone and the planting season for each vegetable. Different vegetables thrive in different temperatures, so it's essential to choose varieties that are well-suited for your region.

Take note of each vegetable's specific growing requirements, such as spacing, water needs, and sunlight preferences. This information is typically available on seed packets or can be found in gardening books or online resources.

## 1.4 Planting and Caring for Your Vegetables

Before planting your vegetables, it's important to plan out your garden. Determine the placement of each type of vegetable, considering factors like plant height, shade requirements, and companion planting principles.

When planting your seeds or seedlings, follow the instructions provided on the packaging or consult reliable gardening resources. Some plants are best suited for direct sowing, while others benefit from being started indoors and then transplanted outside. Be mindful of the recommended spacing between plants to avoid overcrowding, which can lead to reduced airflow and increased susceptibility to diseases.

Proper watering is crucial for the health and growth of your vegetables. The general rule of thumb is to provide about 1 inch of water per week, either through rainfall or irrigation. Watering deeply and infrequently encourages robust root growth and helps your plants withstand dry spells.

To keep weeds at bay and conserve soil moisture, consider adding a layer of organic mulch around your vegetable plants. Mulch can be made from straw, leaves, grass clippings, or wood chips, and it acts as a natural weed barrier while also regulating soil temperature.

**1.5 Pest and Disease Management**

Just like any other living organisms, vegetables are susceptible to pests and diseases. It's essential to monitor your garden regularly and take proactive measures to prevent or manage any issues that may arise.

To deter common pests, consider using natural methods such as companion planting, where certain plants repel pests or attract beneficial insects that help control pests. Additionally, regular inspection of your plants can help you identify any signs of infestation early on, allowing you to take appropriate action.

When it comes to diseases, prevention is key. Practice good hygiene by sanitizing your gardening tools, avoid overwatering, and provide adequate airflow between plants. If you notice any signs of disease, such as spots or wilting, consult a gardening expert or your local extension office for proper diagnosis and treatment options.

## 1.6 Harvesting and Enjoying the Fruits of Your Labor

The reward of vegetable gardening comes with the joy of harvesting and enjoying the delicious produce you've grown. Each vegetable has different criteria for determining when it's ready to be picked, so familiarize yourself with these guidelines to ensure optimal flavor and quality.

When harvesting, use clean, sharp tools to avoid damaging the plants. Some vegetables, like tomatoes and cucumbers, are best when picked fully ripe, while others, such as lettuce and spinach, are most flavorful when harvested young and tender. Enjoy the fruits of your labor in fresh salads, flavorful stir-fries, or as ingredients in your favorite recipes.

Chapter 1 has provided you with a comprehensive overview of the basics of vegetable gardening. From selecting the perfect spot to harvesting your bounty, each step is crucial for a successful and rewarding gardening experience. Remember, gardening is a continual learning process, and with practice and dedication, your skills will flourish along with your vegetable garden. In the upcoming chapters, we will delve deeper into more advanced techniques to elevate your gardening knowledge and take your vegetable garden to new heights.

# Getting Started with Gardening

Gardening is a fulfilling and rewarding hobby that not only beautifies our surroundings but also brings us closer to nature. Whether you have a large backyard, a small balcony, or even just a windowsill, gardening allows us to nurture and care for plants, providing a sense of tranquility and purpose. In this chapter, we will explore the basics of getting started with gardening, from understanding soil composition to choosing the right plants for your space. So, roll up your sleeves, grab your tools, and let's embark on this exciting gardening journey together!

**Section 1: Preparing Your Garden**

**1. Assessing Your Space:**

Before diving into gardening, it's important to assess the available space you have. Whether you have an outdoor garden, a balcony, or even an indoor area, understanding the limitations of your space will help you plan accordingly. Take note of the amount of sunlight your space receives; different plants have varying light requirements, and this will influence which ones you can grow successfully.

**2. Soil Composition:**

Understanding the soil composition in your garden is crucial for healthy plant growth. The three main types of soil are clay, sandy, and loamy. Clay soil can be dense and hold water, while sandy soil drains quickly. Loamy soil, which is a balanced mixture, is generally considered ideal for most plants. All soils can be improved with organic matter, such as compost or well-rotted manure, which help to improve drainage, fertility, and overall soil structure.

**3. Clearing and Preparing the Ground:**

Once you know your space and soil composition, it's time to clear and prepare the ground. Remove any existing weeds or vegetation from the area to avoid competition for nutrients. Prepare the soil by loosening it with a garden fork or tiller, removing rocks, and incorporating organic matter. This will provide a healthy foundation for your plants to grow.

**Section 2: Choosing the Right Plants**

**1. Understanding Your Climate:**

Different regions have varying climates, and it's important to choose plants that are suitable for your specific climate. Consider factors such as temperature, rainfall, and frost patterns. Research local gardening resources or consult with experienced gardeners in your area to determine which plants thrive in your climate.

**2. Annuals vs. Perennials:**

Choosing between annuals and perennials is an important decision when planning your garden. Annual plants complete their life cycle within a year, while perennials live for many years. Annuals are great for providing colorful blooms all season, while perennials offer lasting beauty but may require more maintenance. A combination of both can create a balanced and dynamic garden.

### 3. Plant Sizes and Spacing:

Consider the ultimate size of your chosen plants when planning your garden layout. Some plants may grow tall, while others may spread wide. Allow enough space between plants to avoid overcrowding, which can lead to poor growth and disease. Additionally, consider the height of plants when arranging your garden to ensure taller varieties don't shade smaller ones.

### Section 3: Starting from Seeds or Seedlings

### 1. Starting from Seeds:

Growing plants from seeds allows for a more cost-effective and rewarding gardening experience. Begin by selecting high-quality seeds from reputable sources. Follow the instructions on the seed packets, which provide essential information like planting depth, preferred temperature, and germination time. Seeds can be started indoors or directly sown into the ground, depending on the plant's specific requirements.

### 2. Utilizing Seedlings:

Seedlings, or young plants, can be purchased from nurseries or obtained through plant swaps with fellow gardeners. This option provides a head start, as seedlings have already germinated and established their root systems. Carefully transplant seedlings into your garden, ensuring they are acclimated to outdoor conditions gradually to prevent shock. Water newly transplanted seedlings well to stimulate root growth and ensure their success.

**Section 4: Basic Gardening Techniques**

**1. Watering:**

Proper watering is essential for plant health. The frequency and amount of water needed vary based on plant species, soil type, climate, and time of year. As a general rule, water deeply but infrequently, allowing the top few inches of soil to dry between watering sessions. Water at the base of plants to avoid wetting the leaves, which can contribute to disease.

**2. Mulching:**

Mulching can greatly benefit your garden by reducing weed growth, conserving moisture, and regulating soil temperature. Organic mulches, such as straw, wood chips, or shredded leaves, break down over time and add valuable nutrients to the soil. Apply mulch around established plants, ensuring it doesn't directly touch their stems to avoid rot or disease.

**3. Pruning and Deadheading:**

Pruning is the process of removing selective parts of a plant, such as branches or leaves, to encourage healthy growth and shape. Deadheading involves removing spent or faded flowers to promote further blooming. Proper pruning techniques depend on the specific plant, and it's crucial to research each plant's pruning needs to avoid damage.

**4. Fertilizing:**

To keep plants healthy and vibrant, it's important to provide them with essential nutrients. Fertilizers can be organic, such as compost or manure, or commercially available synthetic ones. Understand the nutrient requirements of your plants and fertilize accordingly, following package instructions. Over-fertilization can harm plants, so it's essential to strike the right balance.

In this chapter, we covered the fundamentals of getting started with gardening, from preparing the ground to selecting the right plants and utilizing basic gardening techniques.

Gardening allows us to connect with nature, enhance our surroundings, and reap the rewards of nurturing and caring for living organisms. Now equipped with the knowledge to begin your gardening journey, move forward with confidence, and embrace the joys of creating your own vibrant and flourishing garden.

# Preparing the Soil

In the great journey of cultivating a fruitful garden, there exists a crucial step that sets the foundation for all the growth and abundance to come - preparing the soil. This often overlooked and underestimated task is of utmost importance, for without a healthy and nourishing environment, any attempt at gardening is doomed to wither away. In this chapter, we shall delve into the intricacies of soil preparation, exploring the various techniques, tools, and considerations that must be taken into account to ensure a successful harvest.

## 1.1 The Essence of Soil Preparation

Imagine building a house without a sturdy foundation - it would crumble and collapse under the pressures of time and weather. Similarly, a garden without well-prepared soil would struggle to sustain and nourish the plants that grow within it. Soil preparation is the art of creating an ideal environment for plant growth by optimizing factors such as drainage, nutrient content, and structure.

One might ask, why is soil preparation so crucial? The answer lies in the intricate relationship between plants and their environment. Plants draw nutrients and water from the soil, enabling them to undertake vital processes such as photosynthesis and growth. When the soil lacks essential nutrients or has poor drainage, plants suffer from malnourishment, disease, or even death. Thus, by taking the time to prepare the soil, gardeners can provide a rich and stable foundation for their plants, ensuring a bountiful harvest.

## 1.2 Assessing Soil Composition

The first step in preparing the soil is understanding its composition. Soil can vary significantly from one location to another, and even within a given garden, different areas may possess distinct characteristics. By assessing the soil composition, gardeners can tailor their preparation techniques to the specific needs of the plants they wish to grow.

To evaluate the soil, there are several easy and practical methods at the gardener's disposal. The simplest technique is visual inspection, paying attention to color, texture, and structure. Dark, crumbly soil indicates high organic matter content, while sandy or clayey soil suggests the need for improvement. Additionally, by using a soil testing kit, available at local garden centers, gardeners can measure the pH level, nutrient content, and mineral composition of their soil. These tests provide valuable insights into the essential elements plants require for robust growth.

## 1.3 Adjusting Soil pH

One critical aspect of soil preparation is optimizing the pH level. The pH scale measures the acidity or alkalinity of the soil. While most plants prefer a slightly acidic or neutral pH, some species have specific pH preferences. Adjusting the soil's pH to meet the desired range allows gardeners to create an environment conducive to the chosen plants.

To alter the soil's pH, various amendments can be incorporated. For example, to lower the pH in alkaline soil, gardeners can add organic matter like compost, peat moss, or elemental sulfur. Conversely, raising the pH of acidic soil may involve incorporating lime or wood ashes. It is essential to follow the instructions provided by soil testing kits or consult with local gardening experts to ensure proper adjustments and avoid inadvertently harming the plants.

## 1.4 Improving Soil Structure

The physical structure of the soil greatly impacts its ability to retain nutrients, moisture, and provide a favorable root environment. Soils with a large percentage of clay tend to become compacted, impeding drainage and root penetration. On the other hand, sandy soils drain too quickly and struggle to retain necessary moisture and nutrients.

Thus, it is necessary to enhance the soil structure for optimal plant growth. One popular method is incorporating organic matter such as well-aged compost, leaf mold, or manure, which improves both drainage in clay soils and water-holding capacity in sandy soils. Organic matter also promotes the growth of beneficial microorganisms, earthworms, and other soil fauna, further enhancing the soil's fertility and texture.

Additionally, careful consideration must be given to tillage practices when preparing the soil. Excessive tilling can disrupt soil structure, leading to compaction and erosion. Alternatives like minimum tillage or no-till techniques help preserve soil structure, organic matter content, and the beneficial soil ecosystem.

## 1.5 Enhancing Soil Fertility

Fertility is a fundamental factor in ensuring vibrant, healthy plant growth. Fertile soil provides an abundant supply of essential nutrients that the plants need to thrive. When it comes to enhancing soil fertility, there are several strategies at the gardener's disposal.

The primary source of fertility lies in organic matter. By incorporating compost, manure, or other organic materials, gardeners can improve the soil's nutrient content, water-holding capacity, and overall structure. Furthermore, organic matter fuels the growth of beneficial soil organisms that break down organic material, releasing valuable nutrients for plants' use.

In addition to organic matter, supplemental fertilizers can be utilized to address specific nutrient deficiencies. Soil testing kits can identify potential nutrient imbalances, allowing gardeners to apply precise amendments. Balanced fertilizers can be found in numerous forms, including dry granules, liquid concentrates, or slow-release pellets.

## 1.6 Water Drainage and Irrigation Systems

Water, indeed, is the elixir of plant life, and ensuring proper drainage and irrigation is vital in soil preparation. Excessive water retention can lead to root rot and fungal diseases, while inadequate drainage can cause drought stress and hinder nutrient uptake.

The installation of proper irrigation systems, such as drip irrigation or soaker hoses, can help ensure water reaches plant roots efficiently while minimizing the risk of overwatering. Additionally, incorporating organic matter and creating channels or raised beds can facilitate drainage, preventing waterlogging and its detrimental consequences.

## 1.7 Seasonal Considerations

Lastly, it is crucial to consider the timing of soil preparation to optimize plant growth and mitigate adverse weather conditions. Different regions experience distinct seasonal variations, which affect the soil's moisture, temperature, and integrity.

In preparation for planting, it is generally recommended to undertake soil preparation in advance, allowing ample time for amendments to integrate and establish a balanced soil ecosystem. The optimal timeframe often depends on the intended planting season, with some gardeners preparing soil in fall for spring planting or a few weeks before the desired planting date.

The art of gardening lies not only in the nurturing and tending of plants but also in the groundwork laid before the first seed is sown. Preparing the soil in a thoughtful and deliberate manner is crucial to manifesting a thriving garden. By assessing soil composition, adjusting pH levels, enhancing soil structure, and promoting fertility, gardeners can establish the optimal growing environment for their plants. With a solid foundation, plants will flourish, bearing witness to the triumphant rewards of well-prepared soil.

# Understanding Seed Types

Seeds are incredible marvels of nature, containing the potential to grow into vibrant plants, flowers, and trees. They hold within them the blueprint for life, encapsulating all the genetic information necessary to produce an entire organism. However, not all seeds are created equal. In this chapter, we will delve into the fascinating world of seed types, exploring their characteristics, diversity, and the factors that influence their growth and development.

**The Importance of Seeds**

Before we begin our exploration of seed types, let us first ponder the significance of seeds themselves. Seeds are the embodiment of life's resilience, adaptation, and survival strategies. They allow plants to disperse their offspring over vast distances and ensure the continuation of their species. Additionally, seeds have long been vital to humanity, providing sustenance, fuel, and materials for countless civilizations throughout history.

**Seed Structure and Components**

To truly understand seed types, it is crucial to examine their structure and components. At first glance, seeds may appear simple, but their intricate design reveals a wealth of information. A typical seed consists of three primary components: the seed coat, the embryo, and the endosperm.

The seed coat, also known as the testa, serves as the protective outer layer. Created from a specialized tissue called the integument, the seed coat shields the embryo from external threats such as mechanical damage, temperature fluctuations, and pathogens. Some seeds have hard, impermeable seed coats, while others may possess softer, permeable ones.

The embryo is the miniature plant-to-be contained within the seed. Comprising the embryonic root, shoot, and one or two cotyledons (seed leaves), it holds the genetic material necessary for development. The cotyledons provide nutrients to sustain the seedling until it can produce its own food through photosynthesis.

The endosperm, which acts as a nutritional reserve, is a tissue that stores carbohydrates, oils, proteins, and other essential molecules to support early seedling growth. In some seeds, the endosperm is fully consumed during embryonic development, while in others, it remains as a nutrient source upon germination.

**Types of Seeds**

Now that we have a basic understanding of seed structure, let us explore the various types of seeds that exist within the botanical world. These seed types can be broadly classified into two categories: gymnosperms and angiosperms.

## 1. Gymnosperms: Naked Seeds

Gymnosperms, meaning "naked seeds," are among the oldest known seed plants. They bear seeds that are not enclosed within a protective structure, such as a fruit. Instead, gymnosperm seeds are exposed directly to the environment. This class of plants is incredibly diverse and includes conifers, cycads, and ginkgo trees.

Conifer seeds, one of the most well-known examples of gymnosperms, are enclosed within woody cones. These cone scales protect the immature seeds and facilitate their dispersal when they mature. Cycads, on the other hand, produce large, brightly colored cones, while the ginkgo tree features fleshy seeds that emit a pungent odor.

## 2. Angiosperms: Flowering Seeds

Angiosperms, or flowering plants, are the dominant group of plants on Earth, accounting for the vast majority of plant species. Unlike gymnosperms, angiosperms have seeds that are enclosed within a fruit, providing them with an added layer of protection and aiding in their dispersal.

Flowering seeds showcase astonishing diversity in shape, size, and structure. Some plants produce small, lightweight seeds that can be carried by the wind for long distances, while others have heavy seeds that require the assistance of animals for dispersal. The fruits themselves range from dry capsules to succulent berries, illustrating the adaptability and resourcefulness of angiosperms.

## Seed Dispersal Mechanisms

Seed dispersal plays a pivotal role in plant survival and is governed by a multitude of mechanisms. By dispersing seeds away from the parent plant, plants reduce both intra-species competition and the risk of disease transmission. Several organisms, including animals, wind, water, and explosive mechanisms, aid in seed dispersal. Animals, attracted by colorful fruits, feed on them and subsequently disperse the seeds. This process ensures that seeds are transported far from the parent plant, often through the excretion or incidental entanglement of seeds in fur or feathers. Wind dispersal, prevalent in many grasses and trees, allows lightweight seeds to be carried over long distances. Water dispersal is common among aquatic plants, where seeds float until they find suitable conditions for germination. Finally, certain plants employ explosive mechanisms to actively launch their seeds, ensuring efficient dispersal in a limited area.

**Factors Affecting Seed Germination**

Seed germination, the process by which seeds break dormancy and initiate growth, is a vital step in a plant's life cycle. Various factors influence seed germination, determining whether a seed will develop under specific conditions. Some of these factors include temperature, light, moisture, oxygen availability, seed age, and mechanical scarification.

Temperature plays a crucial role in seed germination, stimulating enzyme activity and activating dormant embryos. Each seed species has an optimal temperature range for germination, and deviations from this range can impede or prevent germination altogether.

Light is another factor that significantly influences seed germination. Certain seeds, called photoblastic seeds, require light to initiate germination, while others prefer darkness. Photoblastic seeds may exhibit positive or negative photoblastism, depending on whether they require light or darkness for germination.

Moisture is the key to awakening a dormant seed. Adequate moisture levels are necessary to activate enzymes and facilitate the absorption of nutrients. Conversely, excessively wet or waterlogged soil may drown the seed, inhibiting germination. Seeds also require oxygen for respiration during germination, and insufficient oxygen levels can hinder their development.

Seed age can impact germination rates, as older seeds may exhibit reduced viability due to deterioration or loss of internal tissues. However, some seeds require a period of after-ripening or dormancy before they can germinate, allowing them to synchronize their development with favorable environmental conditions.

Mechanical scarification, or the physical breaking or weakening of the seed coat, is sometimes necessary to overcome dormancy. Scarification can occur naturally through the actions of animals or environmental factors, or it can be artificially induced through techniques like sanding, nicking, or soaking in hot water.

Understanding the rich diversity and intricacies of seed types is essential for anyone interested in the wonders of plant life. From the resilient gymnosperms with their exposed seeds to the impressive angiosperms encapsulated within fruits, seeds offer a window into the remarkable adaptations developed by plants to ensure their survival and proliferation. By comprehending the factors that influence seed germination, we can better appreciate the interplay between seeds and their environment. Seeds, nature's life capsules, have shaped our world, nourishing both our bodies and our souls throughout history.

# Indoor vs. Outdoor Seed Starting

Aspiring gardeners and horticultural enthusiasts are often faced with the dilemma of whether to start their seeds indoors or outdoors. This decision can greatly impact the success and growth of your plants. In this chapter, we will explore the pros and cons of both indoor and outdoor seed starting methods. By delving into the details of each approach, you will gain a comprehensive understanding of the factors that should influence your decision-making process.

**Indoor Seed Starting:**

Many gardeners prefer to start their seeds indoors, primarily due to the controlled environment it offers. Indoor seed starting usually takes place in a greenhouse, seed starting trays, or even a sunny windowsill. Let's take a closer look at the advantages and considerations associated with this method.

**Advantages of Indoor Seed Starting:**

1. Extended growing season: By starting seeds indoors, gardeners can extend the growing season beyond what is typically possible in their climate. This allows for an earlier harvest and can be particularly beneficial in regions with short growing seasons.

2. Pest and disease control: Indoor seed starting minimizes the risk of pests and diseases wreaking havoc on vulnerable seedlings. By keeping plants away from outdoor pests, such as slugs or aphids, you

can significantly increase your chances of a healthy start.

3. Greater control over environmental factors: Indoor seed starting allows gardeners to have precise control over temperature, humidity, and light levels essential for optimal seed germination. Variables such as air circulation and soil moisture can be fine-tuned to meet the specific needs of different plant varieties.

4. Convenient and organized: By starting seeds indoors, you can have all your plants in one location, simplifying care and monitoring. Additionally, organizing your seedlings efficiently can help you keep track of different varieties and ensure each plant receives the attention it requires.

**Considerations for Indoor Seed Starting:**

1. Space limitations: Starting seeds indoors requires adequate space to accommodate containers, grow lights, and other equipment. If you have limited space available, this may be a constraint to consider, particularly if you plan to grow a large number of plants.

2. Equipment and setup costs: Investing in seed trays, grow lights, heating mats, or a greenhouse can add to the overall cost of indoor seed starting. However, this upfront investment can pay off in the long run, given the success rate and advantages it offers.

3. Transplant stress: Moving seedlings from indoor environments to the outdoors can be a stressful process for plants. It is crucial to harden off seedlings gradually before transplanting them into the garden. Failure to do so may lead to transplant shock and hinder their growth.

**Outdoor Seed Starting:**

While indoor seed starting provides an array of benefits, outdoor seed starting also has its merits. Let's explore the advantages and considerations specific to this method.

**Advantages of Outdoor Seed Starting:**

1. Natural environmental conditions: By planting seeds directly in the ground, you expose them to natural sunlight, temperature variations, and wind from the beginning. This can lead to sturdier plants, more adaptable to the outdoor environment, and less dependent on controlled conditions.

2. Reduced transplant shock: When seeds are sown directly outdoors, seedlings bypass the transplanting process. This eliminates the potential stress and shock associated with moving indoor plants to outdoor growing conditions, increasing their chances of survival.

3. Cost-effective: Outdoor seed starting requires minimal investment as it primarily relies on natural environmental conditions. This makes it an economical choice for gardeners on a tight budget.

**Considerations for Outdoor Seed Starting:**

1. Vulnerability to pests and diseases: Starting seeds outdoors exposes them to a higher risk of pests, diseases, and adverse weather conditions. Without the protection of an indoor environment, seedlings may become vulnerable and require extra monitoring and care.

2. Limited control over environmental factors: Unlike indoor seed starting, outdoor gardening is subject to the whims of Mother Nature. Gardeners must rely on weather patterns and adapt their

methods accordingly. This lack of control can be challenging if your region experiences erratic weather or unfavorable growing conditions.

3. Shorter growing season: Depending on your geographical location, outdoor seed starting may limit your growing season. In regions with short summers or harsh winters, it may be difficult to achieve the desired plant maturity before the weather turns unfavorable.

Deciding between indoor and outdoor seed starting ultimately comes down to your specific gardening goals, available resources, and the region in which you garden. Both methods have their advantages and considerations, and the choice depends on factors such as time, space, budget, and personal preference. Some gardeners may opt for a combination of both, leveraging the strengths of each approach. Whatever path you choose, understanding the nuances and trade-offs associated with indoor and outdoor seed starting will equip you to make informed decisions and set your garden up for success.

# Proper Seed Planting Techniques

The success of a garden largely relies on the careful and proper planting of seeds. Whether you have a spacious backyard or just a small balcony, understanding the fundamental techniques for seed planting is essential to foster healthy growth and maximize your garden's potential. In this chapter, we will delve into the world of seeds, exploring everything from seed selection and preparation, to the actual planting process, and the aftercare necessary for successful germination and growth. So, grab your gardening gloves, and let's unearth the secrets to proper seed planting techniques!

**Section 1: Seed Selection**

Selecting the right seeds for your garden is a crucial first step towards successful seed planting. With numerous options available, it's important to consider factors such as soil type, climate, and the amount of sunlight your garden receives. Here are a few key points to keep in mind:

**1.1 Understanding Seed Types:**

Seeds come in different forms, including open-pollinated, heirloom, and hybrid varieties. Open-pollinated seeds are pollinated naturally, ensuring that the offspring will resemble the parent plant. Heirloom seeds are open-pollinated, unique varieties that have been carefully preserved and handed down through generations. Hybrid seeds, on the other hand, are cross-pollinated to create plants with specific traits like disease resistance or increased yield.

## 1.2 Soil and Climate Considerations:

Different seeds have varying soil and climate requirements. Some plants prefer well-drained soil, while others thrive in moisture-retentive soil. Understanding your garden's soil composition and pH level is crucial for selecting seeds that will flourish. Similarly, consider the climate in your region – be it hot and arid, cool and moist, or any other type – and choose seeds accordingly to ensure your plants can withstand local weather conditions.

## 1.3 Sunlight Requirements:

Most plants require a specific amount of sunlight to grow and thrive. Observe your garden and identify areas that receive full sun, partial shade, or full shade. This information will help you select seeds that are best suited for each area, ensuring optimal growth and development.

## Section 2: Seed Preparation

Once you've selected the ideal seeds for your garden, it's time to prepare them for planting. Proper seed preparation can significantly contribute to germination success rates. Let's explore a few important steps in this process:

**2.1 Seed Soaking:**

Some seeds benefit from a process called soaking. This involves
submerging the seeds in water for a specific period, allowing them to
absorb moisture and kickstart the germination process. Seeds with
hard shells, like beans or peas, greatly benefit from soaking, as it
softens the outer layer and enables easier sprouting.

**2.2 Scarification:**

Scarification is a technique used for seeds with hard, impermeable
outer coats. By either scraping or nicking the seed coat, you create
tiny openings through which water can penetrate, enhancing the
germination process. Examples of seeds that may require
scarification include morning glory or sweet pea seeds.

**2.3 Stratification:**

Certain seeds require a period of cold dormancy, known as
stratification, to mimic natural winter conditions. This technique is
commonly employed for seeds native to cold climates. To stratify
seeds, place them in a moist medium, such as damp peat moss or
sand, and store them in a cool environment, such as a refrigerator,
for a specified duration. This process is essential for encouraging
germination in plants like some wildflowers or fruit trees.

**Section 3: Seed Planting Techniques**

Now that your seeds are well-prepared, it's time to put them in their new home—the soil. Proper seed planting techniques ensure that seeds have the best chance of developing into healthy plants. Let's explore some essential steps for successful seed planting:

**3.1 Soil Preparation:**

Prepare the soil by removing any debris and loosening it to a depth of at least 6 inches. Clear away any weeds or competing vegetation, as they can hinder the growth of your newly planted seeds.

**3.2 Creating Seed Beds:**

Creating dedicated seed beds helps ensure proper drainage while maintaining a suitable growing environment. Use a rake or garden hoe to level the soil and remove any large clumps or rocks. This will provide a smooth surface for seed planting.

**3.3 Seed Spacing and Depth:**

Each type of seed requires a specific planting depth and spacing to promote healthy growth. Follow the instructions provided on the seed packet or in gardening references to determine the ideal planting depth. For small seeds, a general rule of thumb is to plant them at a depth three times their own diameter. Proper spacing prevents overcrowding, allowing each plant to access adequate nutrients and light.

## 3.4 Sowing Techniques:

There are various sowing techniques to consider, depending on your preference and the specific seed type. Broadcasting involves scattering seeds evenly over the soil surface. This method works well for small seeds that need minimal depth for germination. For larger seeds, you can create small planting holes with a finger or a dibber, and then place the seeds inside before covering them with soil.

## 3.5 Watering Seeds:

Once the seeds are planted, watering is crucial to initiate germination. Use a gentle misting nozzle or a watering can with a fine rose attachment to avoid displacing the seeds. Water the soil until it is evenly moist but not soaked, as excessive moisture can lead to rotting.

## Section 4: Aftercare

Proper aftercare is essential to promote the healthy growth of seedlings and protect them from potential hazards. Here are a few key steps to consider:

## 4.1 Soil Moisture:

Maintaining proper soil moisture is crucial for the germination and growth of seedlings. Regularly monitor the soil moisture levels and adjust watering accordingly. Avoid overwatering, as it can lead to root rot, fungus, or damping off.

## 4.2 Controlling Weed Growth:

Weeds compete with seedlings for essential resources such as sunlight, water, and nutrients. Regular weeding is crucial to prevent these unwanted plants from overtaking your garden and stunting the growth of your seedlings.

## 4.3 Protection from Pests:

Seedlings are vulnerable to various pests, including insects and small animals. Implement protective measures such as installing fences, netting, or row covers to safeguard your young plants.

## 4.4 Gradual Hardening Off:

Before transplanting seedlings into their permanent growing locations, it's important to gradually acclimate them to outdoor conditions. This process, known as hardening off, involves exposing the seedlings to increasing amounts of sunlight and outdoor temperatures over a period of several days. This ensures they can withstand the transition without suffering from shock or stress.

## 4.5 Transplanting:

Once your seedlings have become strong and well-established, it's time to transplant them to their permanent location. Carefully dig around the base of each seedling, ensuring you retain as much of the root system as possible. Place the seedling in its new hole, firm the soil around it gently, and water thoroughly.

Congratulations! You have acquired the knowledge necessary for proper seed planting techniques. From seed selection and preparation to the actual planting process and aftercare, you now understand the intricate steps involved in fostering healthy growth in your garden.

Remember, gardening is both an art and a science; therefore, don't be afraid to experiment and adapt these techniques to suit your unique gardening environment. With patience, practice, and a green thumb, your garden will thrive, rewarding you with the beauty and bounty of nature. Happy planting!

# Caring for Emerging Seedlings

In the wondrous journey of gardening, nurturing seedlings is a crucial step that demands utmost care and attention. Seedlings are delicate and vulnerable organisms, at the early stages of their development, which require a nurturing environment to thrive. This chapter delves into the essential aspects of caring for emerging seedlings, providing you with the knowledge and techniques necessary to achieve successful growth.

**Section 1: The Importance of Proper Germination:**

Before delving into the intricacies of caring for seedlings, it is essential to understand the significance of proper germination. Germination is the process where a seed begins to sprout and develop into a seedling. During this phase, the seed relies on favorable conditions to awaken from its dormant state, thereby determining the vitality and potential of the seedling.

**1.1 Understanding Optimal Germination Conditions:**

To ensure successful germination, one needs to recreate the natural conditions that seeds require. These fundamental factors include temperature, moisture, and the presence of oxygen.

**1.1.1 Temperature:**

Different plants have varying temperature preferences for germination. Some seeds require warm temperatures, while others thrive in cooler conditions. A thermometer is an indispensable tool to monitor and maintain optimal temperature levels for germination.

## 1.1.2 Moisture:

Moisture is vital to enable the seed to absorb water, initiating the germination process. However, it is essential to strike a balance. Excessive moisture can lead to rotting, while insufficient moisture can hinder germination. Regular misting and monitoring of soil moisture levels are necessary to promote healthy germination.

## 1.1.3 Oxygen:

Seeds need oxygen for respiration during germination. Therefore, soil compaction should be minimized to ensure adequate oxygen supply to the seed. It is advisable to use well-draining soil with good aeration properties.

## Section 2: Providing the Ideal Growing Environment:

Once the germination process begins, emerging seedlings require a conducive environment to flourish and grow robustly. Creating the ideal growing environment involves considerations such as lighting, humidity, and air circulation.

## 2.1 Lighting:

Light is the primary source of energy for photosynthesis, a crucial process for seedling growth. Insufficient light can result in weak and leggy seedlings, while excess light can cause scorching. Balancing the light exposure by providing appropriate durations and intensities is key to successful growth. Utilizing grow lights or placing seedlings near windows with adequate sunlight can help achieve an optimal light environment.

## 2.2 Humidity:

Maintaining adequate humidity around emerging seedlings is vital for their growth. A humid environment minimizes water loss through evaporation and helps the seedlings establish strong roots. Employing a humidity dome or covering trays with plastic wrap can create a microclimate that enhances moisture retention.

## 2.3 Air Circulation:

Proper air circulation around seedlings is essential to prevent fungal diseases and promote healthy growth. Stagnant air can lead to the buildup of excess moisture, creating a favorable environment for pathogens. Gentle air movement can be achieved by using fans on low settings or opening windows periodically.

## Section 3: Watering Techniques for Optimal Growth:

Watering seedlings is a critical aspect of their care, as it directly influences their survival and overall health. However, improper watering practices can lead to root rot, overhydration, or underwatering. In this section, we will delve into effective watering techniques to help your seedlings thrive.

## 3.1 The Importance of Proper Watering:

Understanding the water requirements of seedlings is crucial to prevent water-related issues. Overwatering can drown roots, leading to oxygen deprivation, while underwatering can stunt growth and cause wilting.

## 3.2 Watering from Below:

One of the most efficient methods for watering emerging seedlings is bottom watering. This technique involves placing seed trays in water-filled trays or using capillary mats to allow water to be absorbed from the bottom. Bottom watering ensures the plant's roots absorb water as required, preventing excessive moisture on the foliage.

## 3.3 Consistency in Watering:

Establishing a consistent watering schedule aids in regulating the moisture levels necessary for seedling growth. Monitoring the soil moisture regularly and adjusting the watering frequency and volume accordingly helps prevent over or underwatering.

## Section 4: Providing Nutrients for Healthy Seedling Development:

While seeds contain initial nutrient reserves for germination, as your seedlings grow, providing additional nutrition becomes essential for healthy development. Nutrient deficiencies can lead to stunted growth and compromised overall plant health.

## 4.1 to Seedling Nutrients:

Seedling nutrients primarily comprise macronutrients such as nitrogen (N), phosphorus (P), and potassium (K), along with other essential elements such as calcium (Ca), magnesium (Mg), and sulfur (S). These nutrients are vital for proper leaf, root, and stem development.

## 4.2 Seedling Fertilization:

Applying a balanced and diluted liquid fertilizer can supplement the existing nutrient reserves in the seedlings' soil. It is crucial to follow the manufacturer's instructions and avoid over-fertilization, which can lead to nutrient burn.

Caring for emerging seedlings is both an art and a science. Understanding their requirements and providing optimal conditions for germination, growth environment, watering, and nutrition is key to their healthy development. Nurturing seedlings is a testament to the intricate relationship between humans and nature, in which we shape the foundation for our future harvests. Proceed with enthusiasm, guided by the knowledge and techniques shared in this chapter, and watch your emerging seedlings transform into flourishing plants, filling your garden with beauty and abundance.

# Chapter 2: Cultivating a Thriving Vegetable Garden

Welcome to Chapter 3 of our gardening guidebook, where we dive deep into the art of cultivating a thriving vegetable garden. Whether you're an experienced gardener or a novice with a green thumb, this chapter will provide valuable insights, practical tips, and techniques to help you create a bountiful and rewarding garden filled with nutritious vegetables. So grab your gardening gloves, sharpen your trowels, and let's embark on a journey towards growing your own delicious produce!

**Understanding Your Garden**

Before we delve into the nitty-gritty of cultivating vegetables, it's crucial to understand the nuances of your garden. Every garden has its unique characteristics, including the soil type, exposure to sunlight, and available space. Take some time to evaluate these factors, as they play a pivotal role in determining the success of your vegetable garden.

**Soil Preparation**

One of the first steps towards a thriving vegetable garden is preparing the soil to provide optimum growing conditions for your plants. Start by clearing any debris, rocks, or weeds from the area you plan to utilize for your garden. Next, check the pH level of your soil using a testing kit. Vegetables generally thrive in a pH range of 6 to 7. Adjust the pH accordingly by adding either lime or sulfur to bring it within the ideal range.

Once the pH is balanced, enrich your soil with organic matter such as compost or well-rotted manure. This improves soil structure, enhances drainage, and boosts nutrient levels. Spread a generous layer of organic matter over the garden bed and gently till it into the soil using a rake or garden fork. Aim for a loose, crumbly texture that is conducive to root growth.

**Choosing the Right Vegetables**

Deciding which vegetables to grow in your garden is an exciting yet crucial decision. Consider your personal preferences, climate conditions, and the amount of space available. Some vegetables, such as tomatoes, peppers, and lettuce, are well-suited for smaller gardens or containers, while sprawling plants like pumpkins and zucchini require more space.

Additionally, take into account the growing season and frost dates. Many vegetables can be divided into two categories: cool-season and warm-season crops. Cool-season vegetables, like broccoli, spinach, and carrots, prefer cooler temperatures and can tolerate mild frosts. Warm-season crops, such as tomatoes, peppers, and corn, excel in warmer temperatures and should be planted after the threat of frost has passed.

**Planting Techniques**

Each vegetable has its specific planting requirements. Some vegetables, like seeds, are best sown directly into the garden bed, while others thrive when transplanted from seedlings. It's crucial to follow the instructions provided on seed packets or consult a gardening guide for precise planting depths and spacing.

When sowing seeds directly, create furrows or individual holes using a garden trowel or your fingers. Drop the seeds in at the recommended spacing, cover them with soil, and gently firm the soil to ensure good seed-to-soil contact. Remember to label the rows to keep track of your crops and make maintenance easier.

For transplanting seedlings, prepare a small hole in the garden bed and gently remove the seedling from its container. Place the root ball in the hole and fill the gap with soil, ensuring the top of the root ball is level with the soil surface. Lightly water the plant to settle the soil and promote root establishment.

**Watering and Mulching**

Proper watering is essential to maintain healthy vegetable plants. In general, most vegetables require around one inch of water per week, either from rainfall or irrigation. However, factors like soil type and climate influence the required amount. To prevent excessive evaporation and maintain soil moisture, mulching is highly recommended. Apply a layer of organic mulch, such as straw or wood chips, around your plants, leaving a small gap around the stem to prevent rotting. Mulch not only conserves water but also suppresses weed growth and regulates soil temperature.

**Fertilization and Maintenance**

Regular fertilization ensures that your vegetable plants receive adequate nutrients throughout their growth cycle. Before planting, incorporate a balanced, slow-release fertilizer into the soil according to the manufacturer's instructions. As your plants grow, side-dress them with additional organic fertilizers, such as compost or fish emulsion, to provide a nutrient boost.

To maintain a healthy garden, proper maintenance is required. Regularly inspect your plants for pests and diseases, intervening promptly if any issues arise. In addition, remove weeds that compete for nutrients and space with your vegetables. Be cautious when using pesticides, opting for organic solutions whenever possible to minimize harm to beneficial insects and the ecosystem.

**Harvesting and Enjoying**

As your vegetables mature, it's essential to harvest them at the peak of their flavor and nutritional content. Each vegetable has its specific signs of maturity, such as size, color, or firmness. Consult gardening resources or trust your senses to determine when it is the right time to harvest. Remember to use clean tools while harvesting to prevent the spread of diseases.

Once you've harvested your bounty, the possibilities for culinary delight are endless. Whip up delicious salads, hearty stews, or simply savor freshly picked vegetables as a snack. Homegrown vegetables not only provide incredible taste but also offer superior nutrient content compared to store-bought produce.

Chapter 3 has provided invaluable insights on cultivating a thriving vegetable garden, equipping you with the knowledge and techniques necessary for a successful gardening experience.

From preparing the soil to harvesting the fruits of your labor, we hope this chapter has empowered you to grow an abundant and rewarding garden. Implement these tips, adapt them to your specific needs, and let the joy of nurturing plants and enjoying homegrown vegetables fill your life! Happy gardening!

# Essential Watering Practices

Watering is one of the most essential aspects of maintaining a healthy and thriving garden. While it may seem like a straightforward task, there are various factors to consider to ensure optimal water usage and conservation. In this chapter, we will explore three essential watering practices that every gardener should be familiar with. These practices include understanding watering needs, utilizing efficient watering systems, and implementing proper watering techniques.

**Understanding Watering Needs:**

Before diving into the specifics of watering, it is crucial to understand the water needs of different plants, as they vary depending on their species, size, stage of growth, and environmental conditions. Some plants, such as succulents, have adapted to arid climates and require less frequent watering, while others, like leafy greens, have a higher demand for moisture.

To determine the watering needs of your plants, it is important to pay attention to the soil moisture level. Stick your finger about an inch into the soil near the plant's root zone. If it feels dry, it's time to water. However, if it feels moist, hold off watering until the soil dries out slightly. Monitoring soil moisture will help prevent overwatering, which can lead to root rot and other diseases.

Additionally, consider the weather conditions when determining watering needs. Rainfall can significantly reduce the frequency of watering, while hot and dry weather may increase the frequency and duration. It is essential to strike a balance between supplying enough water to meet the plant's needs without drowning it.

**Efficient Watering Systems:**

Watering systems play a crucial role in ensuring efficient water usage in your garden. Here, we will explore three popular watering systems: drip irrigation, soaker hoses, and sprinklers.

**1. Drip Irrigation:**

Drip irrigation is a highly efficient watering system that delivers water directly to the plant's root zone. This system helps minimize water loss due to evaporation and ensures that plants receive a consistent supply of moisture. Drip irrigation is particularly beneficial for gardens with dense planting arrangements, as it allows you to water each plant individually.

To set up a drip irrigation system, attach a series of tubing and emitters to your main water source. Place the emitters near the base of each plant, allowing water to slowly drip into the soil. Drip irrigation also provides an opportunity to incorporate timers and sensors, enabling automated and precise watering schedules.

**2. Soaker Hoses:**

Soaker hoses are another efficient watering option, especially for garden beds and shrubs. These hoses are made from recycled materials and release water through tiny pores along their length. The water seeps into the soil directly at the plant's root zone, reducing evaporation loss.

To utilize soaker hoses, lay them gently around your plants, making sure they cover the entire root area. Connect the hoses to your water source and turn on the supply at a low pressure. This setup ensures a slow and even distribution of water, promoting deep root growth and minimizing surface runoff.

**3. Sprinklers:**
Sprinkler systems are commonly used in larger gardens or lawns. While sprinklers may not be as water-efficient as drip irrigation or soaker hoses, they can still be optimized to minimize water waste. It is crucial to choose a sprinkler head that produces large droplets, as finer mists are prone to evaporation.

When setting up a sprinkler system, be mindful of the water pressure. High pressure can cause water to disperse unevenly and lead to runoff. Aim to water during the early morning or late evening when evaporation rates are lower, and wind interference is minimal. Regularly inspect and maintain your sprinklers to ensure they are functioning correctly and adjust them as needed throughout the growing season.

**Proper Watering Techniques:**

Watering techniques also play a significant role in promoting healthy plants and water conservation. Here, we will discuss three essential techniques: deep watering, mulching, and avoiding foliage wetting.

**1. Deep Watering:**

Deep watering involves applying water directly to the soil's root zone rather than just wetting the surface. This technique encourages plants to develop deep roots, making them more resilient to drought and heat stress. Shallow watering, on the other hand, promotes shallow root growth, rendering plants more susceptible to water shortages.

To deep water your plants, slowly apply water at the base of the plants, allowing it to penetrate the soil deeply. Water until the soil is moist several inches below the surface. This method may require longer watering times but will reduce the frequency, conserving water and promoting healthier plants.

**2. Mulching:**

Mulching is an effective technique to retain soil moisture, suppress weed growth, and regulate soil temperature. By spreading a layer of organic matter, such as wood chips, straw, or compost, around your plants, you create a protective barrier that minimizes water evaporation from the soil surface.

When applying mulch, ensure a thickness of 2-4 inches, leaving a small gap around the plant stems to prevent rot. Mulch acts as a sponge, absorbing water and gradually releasing it into the soil. As a result, you can reduce watering frequency while maintaining optimal soil moisture levels.

**3. Avoiding Foliage Wetting:**
Watering the foliage of plants is not ideal since wet leaves can promote the development of fungal diseases. Instead, focus on watering the soil directly at the plant's base to reach the roots effectively. However, there are exceptions. Some plants, like ferns or epiphytes, may benefit from misting or a light spray on their foliage to mimic their natural habitat.

When watering, direct the water flow close to the ground, avoiding excessive splashing or runoff. By preventing unnecessary foliage wetting, not only do you reduce the risk of disease, but you also maximize water utilization by directing it where it is needed most.

Watering practices are an integral part of successful gardening. By understanding the watering needs of your plants, utilizing efficient watering systems, and implementing proper watering techniques, you can promote plant health, conserve water resources, and minimize water wastage. Remember, the key to effective watering lies in achieving a balance between providing enough moisture for growth and avoiding overwatering. Happy gardening!

# Feeding and Fertilizing Strategies

In order to thrive and flourish, all living organisms require sustenance. Just like any other living entity, plants also rely on proper feeding and fertilizing strategies to grow and maintain their health. This chapter aims to delve deeper into the crucial aspects of feeding and fertilizing that contribute to the overall well-being of plants. We will explore various feeding techniques, discuss essential nutrients for plant growth, and explore different types of fertilizers that can effectively enhance plant development.

**Section 1: Feeding Strategies**

**1.1 Photosynthesis:**

Photosynthesis is the primary feeding strategy employed by all green plants. It is a complex mechanism through which plants convert sunlight, water, and carbon dioxide into energy-rich carbohydrates, such as glucose. This energy fuels the plant's metabolic processes, enabling growth and reproduction.

During photosynthesis, plants use specialized organelles called chloroplasts, which contain the pigment chlorophyll. This pigment captures sunlight and facilitates the conversion of solar energy into chemical energy within plant cells. This stored energy is then utilized to fuel cellular activities and promote growth.

**1.2 Water Uptake:**

Water is an essential element in plant feeding strategies. Through a process called osmosis, plants absorb water from the soil through their roots. This water is then transported upwards through specialized tissues called xylem vessels, which act like tiny pipes within the plant. Once the water reaches the leaves, it is utilized during photosynthesis and transpiration.

Transpiration refers to the loss of water vapor from plant leaves into the surrounding atmosphere. As water moves through the plant, it carries essential nutrients obtained from the soil, ensuring their distribution throughout the plant's various tissues.

**1.3 Nutrient Uptake:**

Apart from water, plants also require various nutrients for their growth and survival. These nutrients can be divided into two categories: macronutrients and micronutrients. Macronutrients are required in larger quantities, while micronutrients are needed in smaller amounts.

The primary macronutrients include nitrogen (N), phosphorus (P), and potassium (K), often referred to as NPK. Nitrogen is essential for promoting leafy growth, phosphorus aids in root development, and potassium enhances overall plant health and disease resistance.

In addition to macronutrients, plants also need other elements like calcium, magnesium, and sulfur in relatively larger amounts, further contributing to their nutritional requirements.

**Section 2: Fertilizing Strategies**

**2.1 Organic Fertilizers:**

Organic fertilizers are derived from natural sources, such as animal manure, compost, or decomposed plant matter. These fertilizers release nutrients slowly and improve the soil structure by increasing its organic matter content.

One popular organic-fertilizer choice is compost, which is created by allowing organic materials to decompose over time. Compost provides a rich source of nutrients, improves soil water-holding capacity, and promotes the growth of beneficial microorganisms, creating a sustainable and balanced ecosystem within the soil.

Another widely used organic fertilizer is manure. Animal manure, rich in essential nutrients, enhances soil fertility and promotes healthy plant growth. However, it is essential to properly compost or age manure before application to prevent the risk of burning plants due to excessive nutrient concentration.

**2.2 Inorganic Fertilizers:**

Inorganic or synthetic fertilizers are artificially manufactured products produced using chemical processes. These fertilizers provide essential nutrients in concentrated and readily available forms, ensuring rapid plant uptake.

Inorganic fertilizers typically contain varying concentrations of nitrogen (N), phosphorus (P), and potassium (K), commonly marked as NPK ratios. The ratios indicate the relative quantities of each nutrient present in the fertilizer.

While synthetic fertilizers provide immediate nutrient availability, their excessive or improper use can lead to adverse effects. Overuse may result in nutrient imbalances, environmental pollution, and altered microbial activity in the soil, thereby impacting the overall soil health.

## 2.3 Controlled-Release Fertilizers:

Controlled-release fertilizers offer a more balanced and gradual nutrient release to match the plant's requirements over an extended period. These fertilizers usually consist of coated granules or pellets that slowly release nutrients as they break down in response to environmental conditions.

The controlled-release characteristic of these fertilizers helps prevent nutrient loss due to leaching and enhances nutrient-use efficiency. By slowly releasing nutrients, plants can take up the required amounts without excessive nutrient surpluses or deficiencies.

These fertilizers are particularly useful in large-scale agriculture, nursery production, and turf management, as they reduce the frequency of nutrient applications and minimize labor-intensive fertilization practices.

**Section 3: Efficient Fertilization Practices**

**3.1 Soil Testing:**

Before applying fertilizers, it is essential to understand the nutritional requirements of the soil and plants. Conducting a soil test helps determine the existing nutrient levels, pH, and organic matter content, guiding the selection and application of appropriate fertilizers.

Soil tests are usually conducted by collecting soil samples from multiple locations in the area of interest and sending them to a specialized laboratory for analysis. The results obtained provide valuable insights into the nutrient deficiencies or excesses present in the soil, allowing for targeted and efficient fertilization.

**3.2 Correct Fertilizer Application:**

To ensure efficient use of fertilizers and prevent nutrient wastage, proper fertilizer application techniques are crucial. Here are a few recommended practices:

- Following the recommended dosage: Excessive fertilizer

application doesn't necessarily lead to better plant growth but may harm plants and impact the environment. Adhering to the recommended dosage ensures a balanced nutrient supply without causing harm.

- Proper timing: Applying fertilizers at the right time is essential to synchronize nutrient availability with the plant's growth cycle. Different plants have varying nutrient requirements during different developmental stages.

- Uniform distribution: Fertilizers should be evenly distributed across the target area to ensure consistent nutrient supply to all plants. This can be achieved using appropriate application equipment, such as spreaders or sprayers.

- Avoiding nutrient runoff: To prevent environmental pollution, it is crucial to avoid applying fertilizers when heavy rainfall is expected. This reduces the chances of nutrient runoff into water bodies, minimizing the negative impact on aquatic ecosystems.

Feeding and fertilizing strategies play a vital role in promoting the healthy growth and development of plants. By understanding the importance of photosynthesis, water uptake, and nutrient absorption, we can cultivate a thriving ecosystem within our gardens, farms, and landscapes. Additionally, the selection and application of appropriate fertilizers, whether organic, inorganic, or controlled-release, contribute to sustainable and efficient plant nutrition. By implementing efficient fertilization practices and maintaining a balanced nutrient regime, we can nurture plants to their fullest potential and ensure the long-term health and productivity of our green spaces.

# Weed and Pest Management

As we delve deeper into the world of agriculture, it is imperative to address one of the most significant challenges farmers face today - weed and pest management. Weeds and pests have the potential to wreak havoc on crops, leading to significant yield losses and economic damage. In this chapter, we will explore the various aspects of weed and pest management, from understanding the different types of weeds and pests to implementing sustainable and effective control measures.

## Section 1: The Impact of Weeds and Pests

### 1.1 Weeds: Nature's Tenacious Invaders

Weeds are nature's tenacious invaders that compete with crops for vital resources such as water, sunlight, and nutrients. Their unwelcome presence not only stunts crop growth but also reduces yield potentials. Moreover, some weeds host diseases and pests that can further harm crops, making weed management an essential aspect of modern farming.

### 1.1.1 Types of Weeds

Weeds come in various forms, including grasses, sedges, and broadleaves. Understanding the different types of weeds is crucial for effective management. Examples of common weeds include crabgrass, pigweed, dandelions, and thistles. Each species has its own growth pattern, life cycle, and potency to cause harm, necessitating tailored control strategies.

## 1.1.2 Weed Life Cycles

It is vital for farmers to comprehend the life cycle of weeds to develop efficient eradication plans. Weeds can be annuals, biennials, or perennials, with each category requiring distinct control methods. Annual weeds complete their life cycle within a year, while biennials do so in two years. Perennial weeds persist for multiple growing seasons, making them the most challenging to eliminate.

## 1.2 Pests: Nuisances of Agronomy

Pests pose another significant challenge to successful agriculture, as they can cause substantial damage to crops, leading to reduced quality and quantity. Insects, rodents, birds, and even microorganisms fall under the broad umbrella of agricultural pests. Understanding their methods of attack and lifecycle is crucial when developing pest management strategies.

## 1.2.1 Types of Pests

Pests can vary significantly depending on the region and type of crops. Insect pests such as aphids, caterpillars, and beetles are common threats to agricultural productivity. Rodents such as rats and mice can destroy stored crops, while birds can cause substantial damage when feeding on fruit and seed crops.

## 1.2.2 Pest Life Cycles

Similar to weeds, pests have distinct life cycles that farmers need to understand to implement effective control measures. Pests can be classified as complete metamorphosis (e.g., butterflies) or incomplete metamorphosis (e.g., grasshoppers). Knowing the different stages in pest development, such as eggs, larvae/nymphs, pupae, and adults, is vital for targeted interventions.

## Section 2: Sustainable Weed and Pest Management Practices

## 2.1 Integrated Pest Management (IPM)

Modern agricultural practices emphasize the use of Integrated Pest Management (IPM) to ensure sustainable farming and minimize the reliance on chemical pesticides. IPM combines various control strategies to manage weed and pest populations effectively. These strategies include cultural, biological, mechanical, and chemical methods used in a complementary manner.

## 2.1.1 Cultural Control

Cultural control involves implementing farming practices that limit weed and pest populations while promoting crop health. These practices include crop rotation, selection of pest-resistant varieties, and optimizing irrigation and fertilization techniques. By creating an unfavorable environment for weeds and pests, cultural control aids in minimizing their impact.

### 2.1.2 Biological Control

Biological control aims to utilize natural enemies of pests to limit their populations. This method includes the introduction of predator insects, parasitic wasps, or nematodes that prey on specific pests. By enhancing the population of beneficial organisms, farmers can naturally reduce pest numbers and minimize chemical interventions.

### 2.1.3 Mechanical Control

Mechanical control methods involve physical intervention to eliminate weeds and pests. These techniques include hand weeding, hoeing, cultivation, mulching, and the use of traps and barriers. While labor-intensive, mechanical control can be highly effective, particularly in organic farming systems that avoid chemical treatments.

### 2.1.4 Chemical Control

Chemical control, also known as pesticide use, remains a viable tool in managing weeds and pests. However, it is essential to use chemical control judiciously and responsibly to avoid adverse effects on ecosystems, human health, and non-target organisms. Selective herbicides and insecticides should be carefully chosen and applied following recommended doses and timing.

## 2.2 Herbicide Resistance Management

One of the significant challenges in weed management is the emergence of herbicide-resistant weeds. Over-reliance on specific herbicides has led to the evolution of weed populations that are no longer affected by these chemicals. To counter herbicide resistance, farmers must adopt diverse weed management strategies, reduce herbicide use, and incorporate non-chemical weed control methods.

## 2.3 Monitoring and Early Detection

Building a robust system to monitor weed and pest populations is essential to catch potential outbreaks early. Regular field scouting, trapping, and pheromone monitoring techniques can detect the presence of pests before they cause severe damage. Early detection allows farmers to implement control measures promptly, minimizing economic losses.

## 2.4 Education and Information Sharing

Continuous education and information sharing play a pivotal role in effective weed and pest management. Farmers should stay updated on the latest research, best practices, and novel control methods. Collaborative efforts between farmers, researchers, and agricultural organizations promote knowledge transfer, ensuring improved management results.

Weed and pest management remain integral to successful agriculture, as weeds and pests can significantly reduce crop productivity and quality. Employing integrated and sustainable management practices, tailored to the specific weed and pest challenges, is vital for long-term agricultural sustainability. While chemical control may be necessary, it should be utilized judiciously, considering its potential environmental and health impacts. Through continuous research, education, and collaborative efforts within the agricultural community, the challenges of weed and pest management can be effectively addressed, ensuring food security and economic prosperity for farmers worldwide.

# Providing Adequate Support and Pruning

In the world of gardening and horticulture, one of the keys to successful plant growth and development lies in providing adequate support and regular pruning. Whether you have a sprawling vegetable garden, a charming flower bed, or even a collection of potted plants, giving your plants the support they need and ensuring they receive proper pruning can greatly enhance their health, productivity, and aesthetic appeal.

This chapter delves into the importance of providing adequate support to plants and the art of pruning. We will explore various methods of plant support, the benefits of pruning, and the best practices to achieve optimal results. So, grab your gardening tools and join us as we embark on this journey of nurturing plants to their fullest potential.

**Section 1: Providing Adequate Support:**

**1.1 Understanding the Need for Plant Support:**

Many plants have a natural tendency to grow vertically, reaching for sunlight and spreading their foliage to capture optimal amounts of light. However, certain plants struggle to support themselves, especially those with weak stems, heavy fruiting bodies, or trailing growth habits. In these cases, gardeners must step in and provide the necessary support to ensure their plants thrive.

## 1.2 Types of Plant Supports:

There are numerous types of plant supports available, each catering to specific plant requirements, growth patterns, and aesthetic preferences. Here are a few commonly used supports:

### 1.2.1 Stakes and Trellises:

Stakes and trellises provide vertical support for plants such as tomatoes, peppers, and climbing vines. Sturdy stakes can be driven into the ground, while trellises offer a framework for plants to attach and grow upon. These supports not only help plants stand upright but also aid in proper air circulation and easy harvesting.

### 1.2.2 Cages and Fences:

Cages and fences are versatile plant supports that serve a dual purpose of providing support and acting as a protective barrier. Suitable for climbing plants like peas and beans, tomato cages or metal fences offer stability while allowing plants to grow naturally. Additionally, they act as deterrents for pests and hungry critters.

### 1.2.3 Arches and Arbors:

Often used for aesthetic appeal, arches and arbors provide a grand entrance or focal point in a garden. These supports are mainly employed for vining plants, such as roses and clematis. Once these plants are guided to grow over arches and arbors, they create stunning displays, transforming any ordinary garden into a magical space.

**1.2.4 Netting and Trellis Systems:**

For larger-scale gardens or commercial orchards, netting and trellis systems offer an efficient way to manage plant growth. Netting is used to protect crops from birds or other pests, while trellis structures allow for systematic training and canopy management in fruit trees, ensuring efficient sunlight exposure and air circulation.

**Section 2: The Art of Pruning:**

**2.1 Understanding the Benefits of Pruning:**

Pruning is an essential technique that involves selectively removing plant parts, such as branches, buds, or roots. By removing unwanted or damaged parts, gardeners can promote plant health, stimulate growth, improve aesthetics, and enhance fruiting or flowering. Pruning also allows gardeners to shape plants, control their size, and prevent overcrowding.

## 2.2 Common Pruning Techniques:

### 2.2.1 Deadheading:

Deadheading is the process of removing spent flowers to encourage the production of new blooms. This technique is commonly used for perennial flowers like roses, marigolds, and petunias. By regularly deadheading, plants divert their energy into new growth and continuous flowering rather than seed production.

### 2.2.2 Canopy Thinning:

Thinning the canopy is often practiced in fruit trees to enhance air circulation and light penetration. By selectively removing certain branches, gardeners ensure that all parts of the tree receive adequate sunlight, reducing the risk of disease and improving fruit quality.

### 2.2.3 Crown Reduction:

Crown reduction involves pruning the upper branches of a tree to reduce its overall size or reshape its canopy. This technique is useful when trees become too large for their surroundings or pose a risk to structures. By carefully removing branches, gardeners can control the size and appearance of trees without harming their health.

## 2.2.4 Training and Espaliering:

Training and espaliering are pruning techniques that involve shaping plants to grow in a specific direction or pattern against a wall, fence, or trellis. This method creates beautiful designs while optimizing space and maximizing fruit production. Espaliered apple or pear trees serve as stunning examples of this technique.

In this chapter, we have explored the significance of providing adequate support and regular pruning in the realm of gardening and horticulture. From stakes and trellises to deadheading and crown reduction, each technique plays a vital role in shaping healthy and thriving plants.

Remember, careful attention to plant support and pruning not only improves the overall well-being of your plants but also enhances their aesthetic appeal, productivity, and disease resistance. So, make it a point to support your plants as they grow, ensuring they reach their full potential while creating a flourishing and enchanting garden.

# Chapter 3: From Blossoms to Edible Delights: Flowering and Fruiting

Nature has an exceptional way of captivating our senses and showering us with its bounties. Among its various wonders, flowers and fruits hold a special place in the human experience. In this chapter, we will delve into the captivating journey of flowering plants, from the mesmerizing process of blossoming to the wholesome delights of their fruits. Join me as we explore the intricacies of floral development, pollination, and the incredible transformations that occur on the path from flower to delectable fruit.

**Unfolding the Story of Floral Development:**

As we embark on this chapter, let us first unravel the enchanting process of how flowers come into being. In every plant's lifecycle, the production of flowers marks a significant milestone. These delicate, colorful structures emerge from buds, revealing nature's artistry in delicate petals, vibrant hues, and captivating aromas.

The anatomy of flowers is a fascinating study in itself. At the center, we find the reproductive organs, including the pistils and stamens.

Petals encircle these fundamental organs, attracting pollinators ranging from bees to butterflies and birds. The intricate pattern of petals, the alluring fragrance, and the sweet nectar collectively ensure that animals participate in pollination, facilitating successful reproduction.

**Pollination: A Dance of Symbiosis:**

The act of pollination serves as a perfect example of the interconnectedness of nature. Flowering plants have developed ingenious mechanisms to ensure the transfer of pollen from the male stamen to the female pistil. Some flowers use the wind to drift their pollen effortlessly, while others have evolved to rely on biotic pollinators.

In this chapter, we will primarily focus on the extraordinary partnership between flowers and animals. Bees, for instance, are master pollinators, tirelessly darting from one flower to another, ardently transferring pollen grains. These industrious insects play a vital role in the reproduction of flowering plants, and the process of pollination is mutually beneficial for both parties involved.

**From Bud to Fruit: The Transformation Begins:**

Once the captivating display of pollination concludes, a mesmerizing transformation begins within the plant. The fertilized ovules, nestled within the pistil, develop into seeds, while the surrounding tissues morph into luscious fruits. Nature's artistry is on full display as fruits take various shapes, sizes, tastes, and colors.

The journey from pollination to fruit ripening is a time-laden process, subject to an array of factors. Environmental conditions, water availability, and the particular plant species contribute to the timelines associated with fruit development. Some fruits mature within a few weeks, while others require many months or even years to reach their peak.

**The Delights of Edible Fruits:**

A significant reward lies at the end of this captivating transformation – the tantalizing world of edible fruits. Fruits are not solely meant to satiate our taste buds; they also serve as a critical part of the reproductive strategy of flowering plants. By enticing animals to consume their fruits, plants ensure that their seeds are transported far and wide, often deposited along with a fertilizer package – animal droppings.

The diversity of edible fruits is staggering, ranging from succulent berries to tangy citrus fruits, and from fleshy melons to fibrous apples and pears. Each fruit carries a unique combination of flavors, textures, and fragrances, inviting us to indulge in nature's gift to mankind.

**Nutritional Benefits and Culinary Applications:**

Beyond their tantalizing taste, fruits offer a plethora of health benefits. Laden with essential vitamins, minerals, and dietary fiber, they contribute to a balanced diet and support a healthy lifestyle. Moreover, they are a rich source of antioxidants, which help combat harmful free radicals in our body, potentially reducing the risk of chronic diseases.

The culinary applications of fruits extend far beyond the realm of raw consumption. Cooks and chefs have creatively infused an array of fruits into both sweet and savory dishes, elevating our culinary experiences. From fruit salads and smoothies to fruit-based salsas and chutneys, the possibilities are endless.

**Challenges and Threats:**
As we immerse ourselves in the captivating world of flowering and fruiting, it is imperative to address the challenges these plants face. Climate change, habitat loss, and pollution threaten the intricate dance of pollination and the survival of countless plant species. Recognizing the value of flowers and fruits in maintaining biodiversity is essential as we strive to preserve our natural ecosystems.

As we conclude our exploration of flowering and fruiting, we are reminded of the beauty and interconnectedness of nature. Flowers and fruits not only enthrall us with their delicate splendor but offer sustenance, health benefits, and an array of culinary delights. Through understanding and appreciation, we can work collectively to protect these treasures of the natural world and ensure their preservation for generations to come.

# The Science of Flowering and Pollination

In the intricate tapestry of nature, one of the most mesmerizing phenomena is the process of flowering and pollination. Flowers, with their vibrant colors and intoxicating fragrances, have long been a source of fascination for humans. However, there is more to flowers than meets the eye. Beneath their delicate petals lies a complex world of biology and science that is crucial for the survival of not only the plants themselves but also countless other species on Earth. In this chapter, we will delve into the fascinating science of flowering and pollination, exploring the intricate mechanisms that govern these processes and the incredible interplay between plants and their pollinators.

## Section 1 - Flower Anatomy:

To understand the science of flowering and pollination, we must first familiarize ourselves with the anatomy of a flower. Flowers are the reproductive structures of angiosperms, or flowering plants, and are composed of several distinct parts. The most conspicuous part of a flower is the petals, which are often colorful and serve to attract pollinators. The sepals, located underneath the petals, protect the developing flower bud. Within the flower, there are male reproductive organs called stamens and female reproductive organs known as pistils. The stamens produce pollen, containing the male gametes, while the pistil contains the ovules, which house the female gametes. The sticky tip of the pistil, known as the stigma, is where pollination begins.

## Section 2 - Pollination Mechanisms:

Pollination is the transfer of pollen from the anther of a flower's stamen to the stigma of a flower's pistil. This crucial step is necessary for the fertilization and subsequent production of seeds. There are various mechanisms by which pollination occurs, each with its unique adaptations and strategies.

### 2.1. Insect Pollination:

One of the most common forms of pollination is carried out by insects, including bees, butterflies, and beetles. Flowers that rely on insect pollination typically have bright colors, fragrances, and nectar as enticements. When an insect lands on a flower to feed on nectar, pollen grains stick to its body. As the insect moves from flower to flower, it inadvertently deposits some of this pollen onto the stigmas, facilitating pollination. Some flowers even have specialized structures, such as tubular shapes or landing platforms, to accommodate certain insect pollinators.

### 2.2. Wind Pollination:

In contrast to insect pollination, wind pollination is a less precise method, relying on the wind to carry pollen from one flower to another. Plants adapted for wind pollination often have inconspicuous flowers with no bright colors or strong fragrances. Their stamens produce abundant, lightweight, and smooth pollen grains that can be easily carried away by air currents. Examples of wind-pollinated plants include grasses, conifers, and some trees like oaks and birches.

## 2.3. Animal Pollination:

Apart from insects, other animals such as birds, bats, and even some small mammals also play a vital role in pollination. Plants that rely on animal pollination often have tubular or bell-shaped flowers, adapted to the specific anatomy of their pollinators. For instance, hummingbirds have long beaks that allow them to reach the nectar deep within tubular flowers, while bats are attracted to white, night-blooming flowers with a strong fragrance. Animal-pollinated flowers frequently produce copious amounts of nectar to entice their visitors.

## Section 3 - Mutualistic Relationships:

Pollination represents a remarkable example of mutualistic relationships in nature, wherein both the pollinators and the plants benefit from their association. Pollinators obtain food resources like nectar and pollen from flowers, while plants enhance their reproductive success by ensuring pollen transfer. However, this beautiful symbiosis is not always a harmonious interaction, as some plant-pollinator relationships can be highly specific and coevolved over millennia.

## 3.1. Coevolution:

Plant-pollinator coevolution is a fascinating process in which the traits of both plants and pollinators have evolved in response to each other. Flowers have developed various strategies to attract specific pollinators, while the pollinators have adapted their behaviors and anatomies to efficiently access the floral rewards. A classic example of coevolution can be seen in orchids, which often exhibit elaborate floral structures and rely on specific insect pollinators for reproduction.

## 3.2. Specialized Pollinators:

Certain plants have coevolved with extremely specialized pollinators, to the extent that they rely on a single species for successful pollination. For instance, certain species of Ficus trees have a mutualistic relationship with tiny wasps known as fig wasps. These wasps have coevolved with the intricate flowers of Ficus, developing specialized body parts to access the interior of the fig and pollinate its flowers.

## 3.3. Cheating and Deception:

While most plant-pollinator relationships are based on mutualism, some plants employ deceptive tactics or cheat to ensure their own reproductive success. Orchids, for example, often mimic the appearance and scent of female insects to trick male insects into "pseudocopulation." These deceived pollinators inadvertently transfer pollen while attempting to mate with the deceptive flower, benefiting the plant alone.

## Section 4 - The Importance of Flowering and Pollination:

The science of flowering and pollination is not only a captivating field of study but also holds immense ecological and economic significance.

## 4.1. Ecological Significance:

Flowering and pollination sustain the delicate balance of ecosystems by promoting the reproductive success of plants and maintaining biodiversity. Without pollination, many plant species would not be able to produce seeds, negatively impacting food webs and ecosystems alike. Furthermore, plants provide habitat, food, and nesting material for countless species of animals, making them vital for the survival of entire communities.

## 4.2. Economic Importance:

The relationship between flowering plants and pollinators is also economically valuable. Pollinators, especially bees, play a critical role in agricultural production by pollinating crops. It is estimated that one-third of global food production depends on insect pollination. In addition to food crops, bees and other pollinators contribute to the reproduction of plants used for medicinal purposes, fiber production, biofuel crops, and more. Thus, the decline in pollinator populations poses a significant threat to global food security.

In this chapter, we have explored the captivating world of flowering and pollination. From the intricate structures of flowers to the complex strategies employed by plants and pollinators, the science behind these processes offers a glimpse into the wonders of nature. The interdependence between plants and their pollinators not only ensures the continuation of species but also shapes entire ecosystems and sustains human life. Understanding and appreciating the science of flowering and pollination is crucial for fostering conservation efforts, maximizing agricultural productivity, and protecting the delicate balance of our natural world.

# Ensuring Fruit Set and Development

In the world of horticulture, the successful development of fruit is paramount to the overall success of any fruit-bearing plant or tree. Fruit set, which refers to the process of flower fertilization and subsequent fruit initiation, is a critical stage that marks the beginning of the reproductive cycle in many plants. It is an intricate process that involves various factors, including environmental conditions, pollination, and the plant's physiological state. This chapter aims to explore the essential elements required for ensuring efficient fruit set and development.

**Optimal Environmental Conditions**

Environmental conditions play a crucial role in initiating and facilitating successful fruit set. Temperature, humidity, light, and availability of water are all key factors that must be carefully considered to optimize fruit development.

Temperature: Fruit set usually occurs within a specific temperature range, as extreme temperatures can have detrimental effects. Warmer temperatures can negatively impact pollen germination and fertilization, while frost or cold weather can lead to flower damage. Growers must consider the optimum temperature range for their specific plant variety and make necessary adaptations to maintain ideal conditions during the critical fruit set stage.

Humidity: Adequate humidity levels are essential for ensuring successful fruit set. Insufficient humidity can hinder pollen tube growth and reduce pollen viability. Growers must strike a balance between humidity levels to promote optimal fruit set without encouraging the growth of fungal diseases or excess moisture-related issues.

Light: Light is another crucial factor in fruit set and development. Different plants have varying light requirements, and some even require specific light exposure durations to initiate the flowering process. Understanding the light needs of specific plant varieties and providing appropriate lighting conditions can significantly enhance fruit set success.

Water: Sufficient water availability is vital for supporting fruit set and development. Inadequate water supply can result in reduced pollen tube growth and inadequate nutrient uptake by the plant. Additionally, fluctuations in water availability can negatively impact fruit quality and overall yield. It is crucial for growers to ensure proper irrigation practices, accounting for the specific water requirements of the plant species, to optimize fruit set and development.

**Pollination and Pollinators**

Successful pollination is a significant determinant of fruit set. Pollination, whether through wind, insects, or other means, facilitates the transfer of pollen from the male parts (anthers) to the female parts (stigma) of flowers. This process triggers fertilization, leading to fruit initiation.

Many fruiting plants rely on pollinators, such as bees, butterflies, birds, and bats, to transfer pollen between flowers. Ensuring a diverse and abundant population of these pollinators is crucial for maximizing fruit set. Growers can create pollinator-friendly environments by planting flowers that attract and provide food sources for pollinators, avoiding the use of pesticides harmful to beneficial insects, and providing nesting habitats or shelter for them.

However, not all plants depend on external pollinators. Some are self-pollinating or have mechanisms in place to facilitate pollination on their own. Nevertheless, careful attention must be paid to ensure proper pollen transfer within the plant or tree, including considerations such as adequate airflow or gently shaking the flowers to stimulate pollen movement.

**Physiological Factors Affecting Fruit Set**

In addition to environmental conditions and pollination, various physiological factors influence fruit set and its subsequent development. Understanding these factors can help growers intervene and optimize fruit set success.

Stress Factors: Plants exposed to stress, whether due to nutrient deficiencies, disease, or adverse weather conditions, often experience reduced fruit set. Stress can affect a plant's hormonal balance, ultimately impacting flower development and success. It is crucial for growers to provide optimal care to their plants, addressing nutritional deficiencies, managing diseases, and ensuring stress-free growing conditions.

Hormones: Plant hormones, including auxins, gibberellins, and cytokinins, play critical roles in flower and fruit development. Appropriate hormonal balance is necessary for proper flower differentiation, fertilization, and fruit set. Some growers adopt hormone application techniques, such as foliar sprays, to support hormonal activity and enhance fruit set success.

Thinning: In certain cases, growers may have to intervene by manually thinning the excess fruit. This practice is particularly crucial when plants experience heavy fruit set, leading to a potential strain on the plant and reduced fruit quality. By removing excess fruits, growers can redirect energy and nutrients towards the remaining fruit, encouraging healthier development and better overall yield.

Successful fruit set and development are essential for high-quality fruit production. By understanding and optimizing environmental conditions, facilitating effective pollination, and considering the physiological factors at play, growers can enhance the odds of a successful fruit set. Each plant species may have specific requirements, and attentiveness to these details is crucial for each grower's success. By implementing appropriate practices and interventions, growers can increase their chances of achieving optimal fruit set and development, ensuring bountiful and flavorful harvests.

# Dealing with Blossom Drop and Fruit Problems

In the vast and rewarding world of gardening, few things can be as disheartening as witnessing the premature dropping of blossoms or the failure of fruit to set. These issues, commonly referred to as blossom drop and fruit problems, can frustrate even the most experienced gardeners. However, fear not, for this chapter will delve into the causes and solutions of these problems, empowering you to overcome these challenges and reap a bountiful harvest.

**Understanding Blossom Drop:**

Blossom drop, as the name suggests, refers to the early falling of flower buds before they have a chance to develop into mature fruit. This phenomenon can affect various flowering plants, including fruit trees, vegetables, and ornamental plants. Its causes can be grouped into several categories, including environmental and cultural factors, as well as physiological and pollination issues.

**Environmental Factors:**

One of the leading causes of blossom drop is unfavorable weather conditions. Extreme temperatures, both hot and cold, can disrupt the process of pollination and fertilization, resulting in blossom drop. For example, excessively high temperatures can cause the pollen to become inactive, interfering with the pollination process. Conversely, cold weather can prevent bees and other pollinators from being active, leading to reduced fruit set. Furthermore, fluctuations in humidity levels can also have detrimental effects on blossom retention, especially in areas with high humidity or dry climates.

**Cultural Factors:**

Cultural practices play a significant role in blossom retention. Improper soil moisture levels, for instance, can impede the plants' ability to absorb necessary nutrients, resulting in weak flowers that are more prone to dropping. Overwatering or underwatering can also disrupt the balance of hormones needed for successful flowering and fruit setting. Similarly, inadequate nutrition, such as nutrient deficiencies or imbalances, can hinder the plants' reproductive capabilities.

**Physiological Factors:**

Plants have an intricate reproductive system that relies on a finely tuned balance of hormones. Any disruptions to this delicate equilibrium can result in blossom drop. Ethylene, a naturally occurring hormone, can be both a friend and foe. While the appropriate levels of ethylene are necessary for floral development, elevated levels can trigger the premature abscission (shedding) of blossoms. Stress, such as drought or disease, can prompt the release of excess ethylene, leading to blossom drop. Additionally, poor vascular health, often caused by root damage or nutrient deficiencies, can impair the plants' ability to nourish and support their flowers, causing them to drop prematurely.

**Pollination Issues:**

For plants that rely on pollination for fruit set, inadequate pollination can be a leading cause of blossom drop. Factors such as a lack of pollinators, insufficient or ineffective pollination, or incompatible pollen sources can all contribute to the problem. In some cases, self-pollination may be necessary, and plants might not possess this ability, requiring the presence of multiple compatible varieties for successful fruit set.

**Solutions to Blossom Drop:**

Overcoming blossom drop requires a thorough understanding of the underlying causes. By addressing the specific factors involved, gardeners can implement a range of solutions to increase fruit set and minimize blossom drop.

**Environmental Solutions:**

To mitigate the effects of adverse weather conditions, protective measures can be taken. Providing shade during extreme heat, using row covers to shield plants from cold temperatures, or creating windbreaks can all help to safeguard flowers and extend the pollination period. Additionally, maintaining consistent temperature and humidity levels in greenhouses or indoor growing environments can reduce the risk of blossom drop.

**Cultural Practices:**

Cultivating healthy plants with a strong root system is crucial to ensuring successful fruit set. Adequate watering, providing a well-draining soil, and monitoring soil moisture levels can all help optimize nutrient absorption and hormone balance. Applying organic fertilizers or amendments that promote flower and fruit development can also be beneficial. Furthermore, regular pruning to enhance airflow and reduce overcrowding can prevent diseases and improve pollination, reducing the occurrence of blossom drop.

**Physiological Considerations:**

To address physiological factors, it is essential to protect plants from undue stress. This can be achieved through proper watering regimes, ensuring plants receive adequate nutrition, and promptly identifying and treating any signs of disease or pest infestation. Maintaining good overall plant health will support the reproductive functions and minimize blossom drop.

**Pollination Strategies:**

To ensure adequate pollination, gardeners can employ a variety of strategies. Creating pollinator-friendly habitats by planting flowers that attract bees, butterflies, and other beneficial insects nearby can help enhance fruit set. Additionally, hand pollination can be employed for plants that struggle with pollination challenges, such as lack of pollinators or incompatible varieties. By gently transferring pollen from male to female flowers, gardeners can increase the chances of successful fertilization and fruit development.

The frustration of blossom drop and fruit problems can be offset by an understanding of their causes and implementation of appropriate solutions. By addressing the environmental, cultural, physiological, and pollination factors involved, gardeners can navigate these challenges with confidence. Armed with a diverse range of strategies, you can now embark on your gardening journey, ready to conquer blossom drop and revel in a fruitful harvest. Remember, horticulture is a constant learning process, and each season brings new opportunities to refine your skills and cultivate success.

# Enhancing Yields through Pollination Techniques

Pollination plays a vital role in the reproduction of flowering plants, contributing significantly to the global production of fruits, vegetables, and seeds. However, natural pollination processes are often influenced by various factors such as declining pollinator populations, environmental changes, and human activities. To mitigate these challenges and enhance yields, scientists and farmers have developed a range of innovative pollination techniques. In this chapter, we will explore some of these techniques and their effectiveness in increasing crop production.

**1. Hand Pollination:**

Hand pollination is one of the oldest techniques used to enhance yields in crops. This method involves manually transferring pollen from the male reproductive organs of a flower to the female reproductive organs. It is commonly practiced in crops like apples, pears, and cucurbits, where inadequate pollinator activity can hamper fruit set and yield.

The success of hand pollination depends on various factors such as the timing of pollen collection and transfer, as well as the correct identification of male and female flower parts. While hand pollination ensures effective pollination, its practicality in large-scale agriculture is limited due to high labor costs and time requirements.

**2. Polyculture and Agroforestry:**

Polyculture and agroforestry involve growing multiple crops together, creating diverse habitats that attract a wide range of pollinators. By providing an ample supply of floral resources throughout the year, these techniques ensure a consistent presence of pollinators, thus boosting pollination rates.

In polyculture systems, the combination of crops with different blooming periods ensures a continuous availability of pollen and nectar sources. Agroforestry, on the other hand, encourages the growth of trees and shrubs in and around agricultural fields, serving as important nesting and foraging sites for pollinators. Research has shown that including diverse vegetation in agricultural landscapes can significantly increase pollinator populations, ultimately leading to improved yields.

**3. Managed Bees:**

Managed bee colonies, such as honeybees and bumblebees, are widely used in agriculture for their efficient pollination services. These bees are transported to fields during the blooming period, ensuring a high density of pollinators when crops need it the most. Managed bees are particularly beneficial in large-scale monocultures where other pollinators may not be abundant or effective.

While managed bees have proven to be excellent pollinators, their use comes with certain challenges. High stocking densities of managed bees can increase competition and aggression, potentially affecting native pollinators. Additionally, promoting the health and safety of managed bees is essential, as they are susceptible to pests, diseases, and the impacts of pesticide exposure.

## 4. Sonic Pollination:

Sonic pollination is a relatively new and innovative technique that harnesses sound vibrations to facilitate pollination. Inspired by the natural behavior of buzz-pollinating bees, scientists have developed devices that emit specific sound frequencies to mimic the vibrations created by these bees. These vibrations release pollen from the anthers of certain flowers, enhancing pollination rates.

Sonic pollination can be particularly useful in crops with tightly closed flowers, such as tomatoes and eggplants, which are not easily accessible to traditional pollinators. While this technique shows promise, further research is needed to optimize the sound frequencies and understand its potential impacts on plant physiology.

## 5. Artificial Pollination:

Artificial pollination techniques involve the use of various tools and methods to manually transfer pollen between flowers. Brushes, cotton swabs, and blowers are commonly used to collect and distribute pollen, simulating natural pollination.

This technique is particularly effective in wind-pollinated crops, such as maize. By capturing pollen from the tassels and applying it to the silks of the same plant or neighboring plants, artificial pollination can increase kernel set and yield in maize fields.

## 6. Pollinator-Friendly Habitat Creation:

Creating pollinator-friendly habitats within and around agricultural fields is crucial for enhancing yields through increased pollinator activity. This can be achieved by planting native wildflowers, constructing nesting sites, and reducing or eliminating pesticide use.

Establishing flowering strips or hedgerows composed of diverse wildflower species can provide abundant food sources for pollinators. Moreover, incorporating nesting sites, such as bee hotels or undisturbed patches of soil, supports the reproduction and survival of pollinators.

Enhancing yields through effective pollination techniques is a pressing challenge in modern agriculture. By embracing a combination of traditional and innovative strategies, such as hand pollination, polyculture, managed bees, sonic pollination, artificial pollination, and pollinator-friendly habitat creation, farmers and scientists can work together to ensure the sustainable and efficient pollination of crops.

Recognizing the importance of pollinators and implementing these techniques not only ensures food security but also contributes to the overall conservation of biodiversity and ecosystem health. Further research and collaboration are necessary to refine and adapt these pollination techniques to diverse agricultural landscapes around the world.

# Chapter 4: Harvesting and Preserving Your Bounty

As the long days of summer give way to the golden hues of autumn, the time to harvest and preserve the fruits of your labor in the garden has arrived. A bountiful harvest represents not only the culmination of months of hard work but is also an opportunity to stock your pantry with nutritious, homemade delights that will bring joy and sustenance to your table during the cold winter months. In this chapter, we will explore the art of harvesting and preserving, sharing time-tested techniques and invaluable tips to ensure that you make the most of your garden's abundance.

**Preparing for the Harvest**

Before embarking on your harvest, it is vital to assess the readiness of your crops. Each vegetable, fruit, or herb has its own telltale signs, indicating when it is prime for picking. While some crops, such as lettuce, must be harvested as soon as they reach maturity, others, like tomatoes or winter squashes, may benefit from a little extra time on the vine to develop their full flavors. As a gardener, it is essential to be attentive and familiarize yourself with the ideal harvest times for each plant in your garden.

Equally important is ensuring that you have all the necessary tools at hand. Keep a trusty pair of secateurs, a harvest knife, and clean baskets or crates ready. It is advisable to have separate containers for different types of produce to prevent cross-contamination, preserve the quality of each item, and simplify the sorting process later on. Additionally, always remember to wear comfortable clothes, a hat, and sunscreen to protect yourself from the sun's rays.

**Harvesting Techniques**

Each plant requires a specific harvesting technique to maximize both its yield and its subsequent growth. Let's delve into some of the most common plants found in a garden and how to harvest them:

1. Leafy Greens: When harvesting leafy greens such as lettuce or spinach, start by removing the outermost leaves, leaving the inner ones to continue maturing. This method, known as "cut-and-come-again," allows you to harvest multiple times from the same plant. Be careful not to damage the central growing point—the heart of the plant.

2. Tomatoes: Gently twist each tomato until it separates from the vine. Alternatively, use a sharp knife or pruning shears to cut the stem about an inch above the tomato. Take care not to bruise or crush the tomatoes during the process to avoid spoiling.

3. Root Vegetables: With root vegetables like beets or carrots, harvest by gently loosening the soil around the plant and pulling the

vegetable straight up, gripping the tops rather than the roots. Remove excess soil, being careful not to damage the stems, and trim off the greens, leaving an inch or two attached to preserve freshness.

4. Fruiting Plants: For crops like zucchini, peppers, or cucumbers, use a sharp knife or pruning shears to cut the stem just above the fruit. Be mindful not to disturb nearby branches or vines, as this can hinder the growth of remaining fruits.

**Preservation Techniques**

With your abundant harvest in hand, it's time to unlock the art of preservation to ensure the flavors, colors, and nutrients of your garden endure long after the growing season ends. Here are some traditional and well-loved preservation methods:

1. Canning: Canning is a reliable technique that allows you to store a wide variety of fruits, vegetables, and even homemade sauces or jams. The process involves heating the food in sealed jars to destroy bacteria and create a vacuum seal. The key to successful canning lies in maintaining cleanliness and following a trusted recipe.

2. Freezing: Freezing is a simple and effective way to preserve your garden produce while retaining its freshness and nutritional value. Blanching vegetables before freezing helps preserve their color, texture, and flavor. For fruits, it is advisable to coat them with ascorbic acid or lemon juice to prevent browning.

3. Dehydrating: Dehydration removes moisture from food, making it less susceptible to spoilage. This method is ideal for herbs, certain fruits, and vegetables. You can use a dehydrator or opt for traditional methods like air drying or sun drying, depending on the climate and available equipment.

4. Fermenting: Fermentation is a traditional preservation method that yields rich flavors, increased nutritional value, and extended storage life. Popular examples include sauerkraut, kimchi, or pickles. Fermenting relies on the action of beneficial bacteria that consume sugars, thereby producing lactic acid. Ensure to use clean equipment and follow proper fermentation protocols to avoid spoilage.

5. Jams, Jellies, and Preserves: Preparing jams and jellies is an excellent way to capture the essence of fruits at the peak of their ripeness. Utilize the natural pectin found in fruits like apples or citrus to create a gel-like texture without the need for added pectin. When making preserves, consider pairing complementary spices or herbs to elevate the flavors.

In this chapter, we have explored the intricate world of harvesting and preserving your garden's bounty. From choosing the perfect moment to pluck each crop from the earth to selecting the most appropriate preservation methods, we hope to inspire and empower you as a cultivating epicurean. As you embark on this journey of harvest and preservation, remember that your garden's yield is a testament to your dedication, patience, and love for nature's rhythms. With each jar of jam, each frozen bag of summer's sweetness, and each delicious meal shared with loved ones, the memories of your garden will flourish, even in the coldest winter days.

# Determining the Right Harvest Time

Harvesting is a crucial stage in the agriculture sector, as it marks the culmination of efforts exerted throughout the growing season. The right harvest time can significantly impact the quality and yield of the produce. Determining the ideal moment to harvest crops requires a deep understanding of various factors and techniques. In this chapter, we will explore the essential considerations, methods, and tools that can aid farmers in making informed decisions regarding the timing of their harvest.

**Understanding Crop Maturity:**

Crop maturity is an important factor when it comes to determining the right harvest time. Maturity refers to the stage at which the crop has reached its optimum harvestable condition, with the highest yield and quality. It is influenced by various physiological, environmental, and genetic factors unique to each crop.

**Physiological Factors:**

Physiological factors play a significant role in crop maturity determination. These factors include the development of reproductive structures, such as blossoms or pods, and changes in color, texture, and flavor. Each crop has specific indicators of maturity, and farmers must familiarize themselves with these signs to harvest at optimal times.

For instance, in fruits, color changes from green to the desired shade, and firmness or sugar content may indicate maturity. Similarly, in grains, changes in moisture levels, kernel hardness, and color can indicate maturity. Understanding these physiological factors is crucial for achieving the highest yields and best quality in harvested crops.

**Environmental Factors:**

Environmental factors greatly influence crop maturity. Temperature, light intensity, humidity, and precipitation patterns all contribute to the growth and development of crops. These factors can vary across different regions and even within a particular growing area.

Monitoring the local environmental conditions during the growing season is vital for determining the right harvest time. It helps in aligning the production cycle with the regional climate patterns, ensuring the crop reaches optimum maturity in the most favorable conditions.

**Genetic Factors:**

Genetic factors also impact crop maturity. Plant varieties have their own inherent growth rates and development patterns, determining when the crop is ready for harvest. It is essential to select suitable varieties adapted to the local soil, climate, and anticipated growing conditions.

Farmers must be aware of the genetic characteristics of their chosen crops and choose varieties that align with their goals, resources, and environmental conditions. This understanding will assist in accurately determining the right time for harvest.

**Harvest Quality Assessments:**

Beyond considering maturity indicators, farmers can also utilize various tools and techniques to assess the quality of their crops before harvest. These assessments provide valuable insights into the crop's condition and help to fine-tune the harvesting timeline.

**Sampling and Laboratory Analysis:**

Sampling involves collecting representative samples of the crop and submitting them to a laboratory for analysis. This technique enables farmers to measure various parameters, such as moisture content, sugar content, nutrient levels, and presence of pests or diseases.

Laboratory analysis provides accurate and quantitative data, allowing farmers to make informed decisions about the ideal timing of harvest. By analyzing multiple samples throughout the field, they can also identify any variations and adjust their approach accordingly.

## Non-Destructive Assessment Techniques:

Non-destructive techniques are gaining popularity in the field of crop quality assessment. These methods allow farmers to evaluate crop maturity and quality without damaging the produce. Techniques such as near-infrared spectroscopy, hyperspectral imaging, and chlorophyll fluorescence can provide valuable insights into the crop's condition.

By using these non-destructive tools, farmers can obtain real-time, on-field assessments, saving both time and resources. This enables them to make more accurate and timely decisions regarding their harvest.

## Visual Evaluation:

Alongside scientific techniques, visually evaluating the crops can provide valuable information. Farmers can observe color changes, firmness, and overall appearance to judge the maturity of their produce. Combining visual evaluation with scientific assessments adds an additional layer of information for determining the right harvest time.

## Practical Considerations:

Besides considering crop maturity indicators and utilizing quality assessment techniques, farmers must also account for logistical and market-related factors while deciding the harvest time.

**Transportation and Labor Availability:**

Farmers must assess their transportation and labor resources to ensure a smooth and efficient harvest. Availability of machinery, such as combines for grains or harvesters for fruits, must be considered. Adequate labor force should also be available to handle the produce efficiently, minimizing any delays or damage during harvesting.

**Market Demand and Price Fluctuations:**

Market demand plays a crucial role in determining the right harvest time, especially for perishable crops. Farmers need to be aware of current market conditions, including demand and price fluctuations. Harvesting too early or too late can have a significant impact on profitability, so farmers must strike a balance between obtaining optimal quality and harvesting at the right time to meet market demands.

Determining the right harvest time is a crucial and multifaceted aspect of agriculture. The interplay of physiological, environmental, and genetic factors, coupled with quality assessments and practical considerations, necessitates careful decision-making. Balancing all these aspects ensures that the crop is harvested at its peak quality and yield, maximizing profitability for farmers. By applying these principles and techniques, farmers can make informed decisions and optimize their harvests, resulting in healthy, high-quality produce.

# Harvesting Techniques for Different Vegetables

Harvesting vegetables is a crucial step that determines the quality and flavor of the produce we enjoy on our plates. It is the culmination of weeks or even months of hard work invested in nurturing the plants from seed to maturity. However, each vegetable varies in its optimal harvest time and requires specific techniques to ensure maximum yield and post-harvest longevity. In this chapter, we will explore the diverse harvesting techniques for a range of vegetables, equipping both novice and experienced gardeners with the knowledge to reap the rewards of their efforts.

## 1. Leafy Greens:

Leafy greens, including lettuce, spinach, and kale, possess tender and delicate leaves that demand a gentle touch during harvesting. The key to harvesting these greens lies in the adeptness with which one cuts the leaves without damaging the plant's growth potential. For lettuce, the outer leaves can be selectively picked as needed, while leaving the inner leaves to continue growing. Spinach can be harvested when leaves are 3-6 inches long, cutting the outer leaves first. Kale, a hardier green, can be harvested by snipping the outer leaves when they reach an adequate size, ensuring the central leaves can mature further and sustain plant growth.

## 2. Root Vegetables:

Root vegetables, such as carrots, beets, and radishes, develop their edible parts below the soil. Harvesting these vegetables requires observing above-ground clues that indicate their readiness. Carrots, for instance, should generally be harvested when they have reached their desired size and color, with the top of the carrot crown protruding slightly above the soil surface. Carefully loosen the soil around the carrot before gently pulling it out. Beets can be harvested when they are roughly the size of a golf ball, grasping the green top near the root and easing it out. Radishes, on the other hand, can be harvested when they have fully grown and can be easily twisted or pulled from the soil.

### 3. Fruiting Vegetables:

Fruiting vegetables, including tomatoes, peppers, and cucumbers, require an understanding of their specific harvesting cues to ensure optimal flavor and texture. Tomatoes, for example, should ideally be harvested when they have achieved full color, whether it be red, yellow, orange, or green, depending on the variety. Slight give when gently squeezed is also an indication of ripeness. Peppers are best picked when they have reached their full color and have a slightly glossy appearance. Cucumbers should be harvested before reaching an excessive size, as overripe cucumbers may taste bitter. Additionally, it is important to regularly harvest fruits to encourage continued production.

### 4. Alliums:

Allium vegetables encompass garlic, onions, and leeks, each with distinct harvesting techniques. Garlic bulbs can be dug up once the leaves start to yellow and wither. Carefully unearth the bulbs without damaging them and allow them to cure in a cool, dry place before storage. Harvesting onions is dependent on whether you desire green onions or mature bulbs. For green onions, select them when the tops are 6-8 inches tall, cutting them at the base. Mature onions should be pulled when the tops naturally fall and begin to dry. Leeks, often used in soups and stews, can be harvested when they reach a diameter of at least 1 inch. Gently loosen the soil and pull them up, removing any damaged outer layers.

**5. Cruciferous Vegetables:**

Cruciferous vegetables, such as broccoli, cauliflower, and cabbage, require a careful hand during harvesting to maintain their integrity and ensure further growth. Broccoli heads should typically have a compact shape, dense texture, and dark green color. Harvesting should be done before the individual florets start to open. Cut the main stem 6 inches below the head to encourage secondary growth. Cauliflower heads should be harvested before they become oversized and begin to loosen. Cut the head off just below the curds, leaving the remaining leaves intact for protection. Cabbage heads should feel firm and solid before harvesting, cutting them off at the base of the stem and removing any loose outer leaves.

**6. Vine Vegetables:**

Vine vegetables, including squash, melons, and pumpkins, require careful attention to harvesting techniques to prevent damage to both the fruits and the vine itself. Squash should be harvested when the fruit has obtained the desired size and color, but before the rind hardens excessively. Cut the squash from the vine, leaving a short stem attached. Melons, known for their sweet rewards, can be harvested when the scent is strong and the stem easily detaches from the fruit. Pumpkins, often associated with autumn, should be picked when the rind is hard and the fruit has reached its full color. Cut the stem, leaving a 2-4 inch length attached.

Harvesting techniques for different vegetables can significantly impact the overall success of your gardening endeavors.

By understanding the specific cues and requirements of each vegetable, one can achieve maximum yield and superior quality produce. Remember to handle the harvested vegetables with care, ensuring their safe transport and storage.

# Proper Post-Harvest Handling

In the world of agriculture, post-harvest handling plays a crucial role in preserving the quality and value of harvested crops. From the point of harvest to the final consumer, the post-harvest handling practices determine the shelf life, nutrient content, and overall marketability of agricultural produce. This chapter will delve into the various aspects of proper post-harvest handling, including the significance, challenges, and effective techniques involved in this essential process.

### 5.3.1 The Significance of Proper Post-Harvest Handling:

From small-scale farmers to large-scale agribusinesses, efficient post-harvest handling practices are vital for maximizing profit and minimizing losses. Every year, a substantial amount of crops are lost due to inadequate handling techniques, significantly impacting both the economy and food security. Proper post-harvest handling not only ensures the preservation of nutritional value and quality of crops but also reduces the risk of contamination and spoilage. Additionally, it increases the shelf life and marketability of agricultural products, enabling farmers to access better markets and attain higher profitability.

### 5.3.2 Challenges in Post-Harvest Handling:

Despite its importance, post-harvest handling presents various challenges that farmers and agribusinesses must overcome. Some of the common challenges include:

1. Time-sensitive nature: Post-harvest handling needs to begin immediately after harvest to preserve the quality of crops. However, this poses a challenge in terms of logistics and labor availability.

2. Infrastructure deficiencies: Inadequate storage facilities, lack of proper transportation systems, and limited access to processing centers are some of the infrastructure challenges that hinder effective post-harvest handling.

3. Pest and disease management: Insects, rodents, and diseases pose a significant threat to harvested crops. Controlling these pests and diseases requires careful attention and appropriate handling techniques.

4. Handling variations: Different types of crops require specific handling methods. Understanding and implementing the right techniques for each crop can be challenging, especially for farmers with limited resources and knowledge.

However, with proper planning, knowledge, and investment, these challenges can be effectively addressed to ensure better post-harvest handling practices.

**5.3.3 Techniques for Proper Post-Harvest Handling:**
To overcome the challenges and achieve optimal results in post-harvest handling, various techniques can be employed. Here are

some effective techniques that farmers and agribusinesses should consider:

1. Harvesting at the right time: Timing is crucial in harvesting to ensure maximum quality and nutrient preservation. Harvesting too early or too late can negatively affect the produce. Regular monitoring and adopting appropriate tools help determine the right time for harvest.

2. Proper handling during harvest: Careful handling during the harvesting process minimizes physical damage and reduces the risks of bacterial or fungal infections. Using appropriate tools and techniques, such as sharp knives and gentle handling, can make a significant difference.

3. Sorting and grading: Sorting and grading produce based on quality, size, and maturity level allows efficient storage, transportation, and marketing. This technique ensures that only the best quality crops reach consumers and reduces losses due to spoilage.

4. Cleaning and washing: Thoroughly cleaning and washing harvested crops remove dirt, debris, and surface contaminants, reducing the likelihood of microbial growth. Water quality, temperature, and proper hygiene practices should be observed during this process to ensure food safety.

5. Proper storage: Choosing the right storage method is crucial for

maintaining the quality and shelf life of crops. Storage options include refrigeration, controlled atmosphere storage, and traditional methods like drying or canning, depending on the crop type. Monitoring storage conditions such as temperature, humidity, and ventilation is vital to prevent spoilage and maintain nutrient content.

6. Packaging: Proper packaging protects crops from external damage and helps retain freshness during transportation and storage. The choice of packaging materials should be based on specific crop requirements, considering factors like moisture control, breathability, and durability.

7. Transportation: Efficient transportation systems and practices are necessary to limit physical damage and minimize the time between harvest and arrival at distribution centers or markets. Well-maintained vehicles, appropriate storage containers, and careful handling during transit play a vital role in ensuring crop quality.

8. Value addition: Adding value to agricultural products through processing techniques such as juicing, drying, canning, or freezing enhances their marketability and shelf life. Value-added products can also access niche markets, generating higher incomes for farmers.

Proper post-harvest handling is an integral part of agricultural production that significantly impacts the quality, marketability, and profitability of crops. While challenges exist, implementing effective techniques, from timely harvest to appropriate storage and transportation, can overcome these obstacles. By prioritizing post-harvest handling practices, farmers and agribusinesses can enhance food security, reduce losses, and contribute to a sustainable agricultural sector.

# Exploring Various Vegetable Preservation Methods

Vegetables are an essential part of our diet, offering a wide range of nutrients and health benefits. However, their freshness and availability can vary depending on the season or geographic location. Therefore, it becomes necessary to find ways to preserve vegetables for extended periods without compromising taste, texture, or nutritional value. In this chapter, we will delve into various vegetable preservation methods that have been practiced for centuries, allowing us to enjoy the goodness of vegetables all year round.

## 1. Canning:

Canning is a popular method of preserving vegetables that involves sealing them in airtight containers under high heat. This process inhibits the growth of bacteria, yeast, and mold, ensuring the vegetables remain safe and fresh. To can vegetables, they are first blanched to stop enzyme activity and enhance color retention. Next, they are carefully packed into clean jars along with boiling liquid such as water, brine, or syrup. The jars are sealed and then processed in a pressure canner or a water bath canner for the required time. Canned vegetables have an extended shelf life and retain their flavor and nutritional profile.

## 2. Freezing:

Freezing is a simple yet effective preservation method widely used for vegetables. It involves subjecting vegetables to extremely low temperatures, which slows down chemical reactions and microbial growth, thereby preserving their quality. To freeze vegetables, they are usually washed, peeled, and cut into desired shapes. Then, they are blanched briefly in boiling water to inactivate enzymes that can cause spoilage. After blanching, the vegetables are immediately cooled in ice water to maintain their texture and color. The drained vegetables are then packed into airtight containers or freezer bags to be placed in the freezer. Freezing allows us to retain most of the nutritional value and taste of fresh vegetables.

## 3. Drying:

Drying, also known as dehydration, is one of the oldest methods of preserving vegetables. It involves reducing the water content of vegetables to a level where microbial growth is inhibited. Drying can be achieved through various methods, such as sun drying, air drying, or using a food dehydrator. Before drying, vegetables are typically washed, sliced, and blanched if necessary. The blanched vegetables are then spread in a single layer and dried until they are crispy and brittle. Dried vegetables can be stored in airtight containers, away from moisture and light. Although the drying process may cause slight nutrient losses, dried vegetables retain their flavor and can be rehydrated for various culinary applications.

## 4. Fermentation:

Fermentation is a traditional method of preserving vegetables that involves the use of beneficial bacteria or yeast to convert sugars into acids or alcohol. The acidity level created during fermentation inhibits the growth of harmful bacteria and extends the shelf life of vegetables. Sauerkraut, kimchi, and pickles are examples of fermented vegetables enjoyed worldwide. To ferment vegetables, they are chopped or shredded and mixed with salt, which draws out the moisture. The mixture is then packed tightly into a fermentation vessel, ensuring all the vegetables are submerged in their brine. Over time, lactic acid bacteria naturally present on the vegetables kick-start the fermentation process. The fermented vegetables can be stored in the refrigerator or a cool, dark place, allowing the flavors to develop and transform over time.

**5. Pickling:**

Pickling is a preservation method that involves soaking vegetables in a liquid, known as a pickling solution or brine, to preserve their texture and flavor. The pickling solution usually contains vinegar, water, salt, and sugar, along with various herbs and spices for added flavor. Pickled vegetables can be acidic, sweet, or spicy, depending on the recipe. To pickle vegetables, they are first cleaned and sliced, and then placed in sterilized jars. The pickling solution is heated to dissolve the salt and sugar and poured over the vegetables. The jars are sealed tightly and stored in a cool, dark place for several weeks to allow the flavors to meld. Once opened, pickled vegetables can be refrigerated for an extended period.

Preserving vegetables through various methods allows us to maintain their quality, taste, and nutritional benefits beyond their peak seasons. Canning, freezing, drying, fermentation, and pickling offer different options for preserving vegetables, catering to individual preferences and culinary needs. By preserving vegetables, we not only reduce wastage but also ensure a diverse and nutritious diet throughout the year. Experimenting with these preservation methods opens up a world of exciting flavors and textures, making our meals vibrant and satisfying regardless of the season.

# Chapter 5: Troubleshooting Garden Challenges

In every gardener's journey, there comes a time when challenges arise. Whether you are a novice or an experienced gardener, troubleshooting garden issues is an inevitable part of cultivating a thriving outdoor oasis. Sometimes, despite our best efforts, plants may encounter difficulties due to various factors such as pests, diseases, weather conditions, or even our own oversights. However, fret not! In this chapter, we will delve into the art of troubleshooting garden challenges, equipping you with the knowledge and tools needed to overcome these obstacles and transform your garden into a flourishing haven of beauty and abundance.

**Identifying and Solving Pest Problems:**

One of the most common challenges faced by gardeners is pests invading their beloved plants. These unwelcome intruders can destroy months of hard work, leaving behind a trail of devastation. The first step in solving pest problems is identifying the culprit. Pests can come in many forms, such as insects, rodents, or even larger animals like deer or birds. By observing the damage patterns, inspecting leaves, and considering the time of day the damage occurs, you can start narrowing down the possibilities.

Once you have identified the pest, it's time to devise a plan of action. Integrated Pest Management (IPM) techniques come in handy here. Instead of relying solely on chemical solutions, IPM focuses on using a combination of cultural, mechanical, and biological control methods. Techniques such as companion planting, encouraging beneficial insects, physical barriers, and regular monitoring can help rebalance the ecosystem in your garden and combat pest issues effectively.

**Conquering Common Diseases:**

Just as humans fall ill, plants can also succumb to various diseases. Fungal infections, viral diseases, and bacterial blights can wreak havoc on your garden, causing discoloration, wilting, or even death of your precious plants. Prevention is key in managing diseases, so practicing good sanitation measures and maintaining healthy soil are crucial.

To prevent the spread of diseases, avoid overhead watering, as wet foliage creates an ideal environment for fungal growth. Furthermore, carefully choose disease-resistant cultivars and maintain proper spacing between plants to improve air circulation. If a disease does strike, swift action is essential. Depending on the disease, treatments may involve pruning infected plant parts, applying organic fungicides, or using biological control methods to combat the pathogens responsible.

**Dealing with Weather Challenges:**

Mother Nature is an unpredictable force that can present a myriad of challenges to your garden. Extreme weather conditions, from scorching heatwaves to frosty winter spells, can stress plants and impede their growth. While we have minimal control over the weather, there are measures we can take to shield our green friends from its harmful effects.

During periods of intense heat, you can employ various strategies to mitigate the damage. Applying organic mulch, such as straw or wood chips, helps keep the soil cool and retain moisture. Additionally, erecting shade cloth or using floating row covers can provide temporary relief to delicate plants, shielding them from the scorching sun. Similarly, during cold snaps, employing row covers and using protective structures like greenhouses or cold frames can safeguard plants from frostbite and harsh winds, extending the growing season.

**Revitalizing Overgrown and Neglected Gardens:**

Sometimes, a garden can become overgrown or neglected, overwhelming both the plants and the gardener. However, with a little patience and strategic planning, such gardens can be brought back to life. The key is to start with small, manageable tasks and gradually work your way through the project.

Begin by removing any dead or diseased plants, clearing away debris, and properly pruning overgrown shrubs or trees. Once you have tidied up, focus on revitalizing the soil by amending it with compost or organic matter to restore its fertility. Next, create a planting plan that takes into account the sun exposure, soil type, and water requirements of each plant. By systematically working through your neglected garden, piece by piece, you can transform it into a vibrant haven that brings joy and relaxation.

Gardening, while immensely rewarding, comes with its fair share of challenges. However, by equipping yourself with the knowledge and strategies to troubleshoot these issues, you can overcome them and nurture a thriving garden. In this chapter, we explored how to identify and solve pest problems, conquer common diseases, deal with weather challenges, and revive overgrown and neglected gardens. Remember, gardening is a continuous learning process, and troubleshooting garden challenges is an essential part of becoming a seasoned gardener. So, embrace the trials and tribulations, and let your love for gardening bloom alongside your flourishing plants.

# Identifying Common Plant Problems

In the world of gardening and horticulture, ensuring the health and vitality of our beloved plants is of utmost importance. However, just like humans, plants can sometimes face various challenges that hinder their growth and development. These challenges can manifest in the form of common plant problems, which can be caused by numerous factors such as environmental conditions, pests, diseases, or even improper care. Understanding and being able to identify these plant problems is crucial in order to provide the appropriate remedies and safeguard the well-being of our green companions.

In this chapter, we will explore some of the most common plant problems encountered by gardeners and plant enthusiasts alike. By the end of this chapter, you will be equipped with the knowledge and skills needed to identify these problems and take the necessary actions to rectify and prevent them in the future.

**1. Yellowing Leaves:**

One of the most frequently encountered plant problems is the yellowing of leaves. When the leaves of a plant start to turn yellow, it generally indicates that there is an issue that needs to be addressed. There can be several reasons behind this occurrence, including nutritional deficiencies, overwatering, underwatering, or even pests.

To identify the cause, one must observe the pattern of yellowing. If the yellowing occurs uniformly across the plant, it may suggest a deficiency in nutrients such as nitrogen, iron, or magnesium. On the other hand, if the yellowing is limited to specific areas or follows a vein pattern, it could be indicative of pest infestation, such as spider mites or aphids. In some cases, yellowing can also point to overwatering, as the excess moisture suffocates the roots, preventing them from absorbing necessary nutrients.

**2. Leaf Spots and Diseases:**

Another prevalent plant problem involves the appearance of various types of leaf spots, discoloration, or diseases on the foliage. Leaf spots can manifest in different forms, typically as small circular or irregularly-shaped lesions of various colors, such as brown, black, yellow, or even white. These spots can be an indication of fungal, bacterial, or viral infections.

To identify the specific cause behind leaf spots, it is essential to consider the pattern, color, and size of the spots, as well as any associated symptoms. Fungal infections often present themselves as brown or black spots, which may be surrounded by a yellow or halo-like area. Bacterial infections, on the other hand, usually result in water-soaked or ooze-filled lesions. Viral infections can cause mottled patterns or yellow spots on the leaves, along with stunted growth.

**3. Wilting and Drooping:**

Wilting and drooping are visual cues that your plants are not receiving the adequate water they require. While underwatering is often the leading cause of wilting, overwatering, root rot, or insufficient drainage can also be contributing factors. Identifying the correct cause is crucial to prevent further damage to the plant.

Observing the overall condition of wilting plants is vital. If the leaves of a plant become limp, wilted, and dry, it likely indicates the plant is not receiving enough water. However, if the leaves are wilted and the tips or margins appear dark or brown, it could be an indication of overwatering or root rot. Additionally, checking the soil moisture level and ensuring proper drainage can help verify the source of the problem.

**4. Pest Infestation:**

Pest infestation is a common problem faced by gardeners and can significantly affect the health and vitality of plants. Various pests, including aphids, scale insects, mealybugs, spider mites, and caterpillars, can cause damage to leaves, stems, flowers, or fruits. Identifying the presence of pests early on is crucial to prevent infestations from spreading and causing irreparable damage.

To spot common plant pests, one must be vigilant and examine plants regularly. Leaf deformities, discoloration, or sticky residue (honeydew) on leaves can be indicators of aphid or scale insect infestation. Tiny webs or stippling on leaves are typical signs of spider mites. Droppings, chewed leaves, or visible caterpillars can suggest caterpillar infestation. Identification guides, such as pest manuals or online resources, can be invaluable in correctly identifying the specific pests and determining appropriate control measures.

## 5. Stunted Growth:

When a plant's growth is not proportional to its age or expected size, it is referred to as stunted growth. Several factors can contribute to this problem, including inadequate sunlight, poor soil conditions, overcrowding, or nutrient deficiencies. Identifying the cause is essential to rectify the issue and promote healthy growth.

To diagnose stunted growth, observing the overall form and development of the plant is necessary. If a plant appears smaller, weaker, or less vigorous compared to others of the same species, it may indicate nutrient deficiencies or poor soil conditions. Similarly, if the plant exhibits elongated stems and smaller leaves, it could be due to insufficient sunlight or excessive competition from neighboring plants. Performing a soil test to assess the nutrient content can assist in identifying nutrient deficiencies and guiding the appropriate fertilization plan.

## 6. Leaf Curling:

Leaf curling, also known as leaf rolling, is a condition where the leaves of a plant exhibit a pronounced curling or rolling shape. This problem can stem from various causes, including viral infections, pest damage, physiological disorders, or even environmental factors such as temperature extremes or drought stress.

To determine the underlying cause of leaf curling, careful observation is required. If the curling is accompanied by discoloration, mottled patterns, or yellowing of the leaves, it could indicate viral infections. Damage from pests, such as aphids or leafhoppers, can also cause leaf curling. Environmental factors, such as excessive heat or cold, can lead to physiological leaf curling. Identifying and addressing the core issue is essential to prevent further curling and restore the plant's health.

Identifying common plant problems is an essential skill for gardeners and plant enthusiasts to cultivate. By familiarizing ourselves with the visual cues and symptoms presented by plants, we can better understand their needs and address issues promptly. In this chapter, we have explored various plant problems, such as yellowing leaves, leaf spots, wilting, pest infestations, stunted growth, and leaf curling. Armed with this knowledge, you are now equipped to recognize these problems and take appropriate measures to diagnose and rectify them. Remember, a healthy and thriving garden begins with a keen eye and a proactive approach towards plant care.

# Addressing Soil and Nutrient Deficiencies

In the world of agriculture, the health and fertility of soil are of utmost importance. Soil serves as a foundation, providing essential nutrients and support for the growth of plants. However, over time, soil can become depleted or suffer from various deficiencies, limiting its ability to sustain productive crops. In this chapter, we will delve into the intricacies of addressing soil and nutrient deficiencies, exploring the causes, symptoms, and most importantly, the solutions to rehabilitate and optimize soil health.

**Understanding Soil Deficiencies**

Soil deficiencies occur when essential elements necessary for plant growth are lacking. These deficiencies can manifest in various forms, affecting the overall health and productivity of the soil. The primary soil deficiencies include nitrogen, phosphorus, potassium, zinc, iron, and manganese deficiencies. Each deficiency exhibits distinct symptoms that can be visually observed, aiding farmers in diagnosing the specific problem.

**Nitrogen Deficiency**

Nitrogen, a crucial element for plant growth, promotes leafy green growth and contributes to protein synthesis. When nitrogen is deficient, plants show signs of stunted growth with pale or yellowish leaves. Such deficiencies are commonly observed in sandy soils or those subjected to excessive leaching; they can also arise from the excessive application of nitrogenous fertilizers. To address nitrogen deficiencies, several strategies can be employed.

One common approach is the application of organic matter, such as manure or compost, which acts as a slow-release nitrogen source. Additionally, the use of nitrogen-based fertilizers, specifically formulated for different crops, can help replenish the soil's nitrogen content. Regular soil testing is essential to customize nitrogen application rates, thereby maintaining a suitable balance.

**Phosphorus Deficiency**

Phosphorus is essential for energy transfer within plants and plays a vital role in root development and fruiting. Deficiencies in phosphorus are often observed in acid soils or areas with low soil organic matter content. Symptoms of phosphorus deficiency include stunted growth, purple discoloration on leaves, and poor root development. Addressing phosphorus deficiencies involves various techniques.

One effective method is to apply phosphorus-rich fertilizers, such as rock phosphate or superphosphate, during the initial stages of crop growth. Soil pH adjustment through liming can also help enhance phosphorus availability. Furthermore, incorporating organic matter into the soil, particularly phosphorus-rich sources like bone meal or fish emulsion, can aid in restoring and sustaining healthy phosphorus levels.

## Potassium Deficiency

Potassium is a vital nutrient that regulates plant water uptake, aids in photosynthesis and cell division, and enhances overall plant vigor. Deficiencies in potassium are often found in sandy or low clay soils, as well as areas with high rainfall or after prolonged periods of heavy irrigation. Symptoms include weak stalks, yellowing leaf margins, and reduced resistance to diseases and pests.

Addressing potassium deficiencies requires the application of potassium-rich fertilizers tailored to the specific crop requirements. Potassium sulfate and potassium chloride are commonly used fertilizers to rectify deficiencies. Crops can also benefit from the application of kelp meal or wood ash, which serve as organic sources of potassium.

## Micronutrient Deficiencies

In addition to the macronutrient deficiencies discussed above, crops may also suffer from deficiencies of micronutrients, such as zinc, iron, and manganese. While these elements are required in smaller quantities, their importance for plant growth and development should not be overlooked.

Zinc deficiencies are frequently observed in alkaline soils and are characterized by stunted plant growth, delayed maturity, and chlorotic leaves. Correcting zinc deficiencies can be achieved by applying zinc sulfate or chelated zinc to the soil.

Iron deficiencies often occur in high pH soils, resulting in interveinal chlorosis, where leaf veins remain green while the surrounding tissue turns yellow. Iron chelate or iron sulfate can be added to the soil to address these deficiencies.

Manganese deficiencies manifest similarly to iron deficiencies and can be corrected using manganese sulfate or foliar sprays.

**Soil Rehabilitation Techniques**

Soil deficiencies are not necessarily shortcomings of a particular soil type, but rather imbalances that can be corrected with proper care and management. Several techniques can be employed to restore soil health and optimize nutrient availability. Some of these techniques include:

1. Crop Rotation: Rotating crops can help break disease cycles, inhibit specific pests, and diversify nutrient requirements, ultimately preventing the depletion of specific nutrients.

2. Green Manure and Cover Crops: Utilizing green manure or cover crops, such as legumes or grasses, can enhance soil organic matter content and nutrient availability. These crops can be incorporated into the soil, enriching it with essential elements.

3. Mulching: Applying organic mulches, such as straw or wood chips, can help improve soil structure, regulate temperature, and retain moisture. Moreover, mulches gradually decompose, adding organic matter and nutrients to the soil.

4. Composting: Composting is an effective method for recycling organic waste and transforming it into a nutrient-rich amendment for soils. Compost improves soil structure, promotes microbial activity, and releases nutrients gradually.

5. Soil Amendments: Various soil amendments, such as gypsum, lime, or elemental sulfur, can be added to adjust pH levels, enhance nutrient availability, and improve overall soil physical properties.

6. Precision Fertilizer Application: Adopting precision agriculture techniques allows for customized fertilizer application, ensuring that nutrients are applied precisely where and when they are needed. This approach minimizes waste and reduces the risk of environmental pollution.

Addressing and overcoming soil and nutrient deficiencies is a critical aspect of sustainable agriculture. By diagnosing deficiencies through visual symptoms or soil testing, farmers can employ a range of innovative techniques to rehabilitate their soil and improve nutrient availability. With careful management and continued monitoring, soil health can be restored and sustained, leading to enhanced crop productivity and ecological sustainability.

# Managing Pests and Diseases Organically

In the world of agriculture, managing pests and diseases is an ongoing challenge for farmers. These unwanted invaders can wreak havoc on crops, leading to reduced yields and compromised quality. While conventional methods rely heavily on synthetic chemicals to combat pests and diseases, there is a growing interest in organic approaches that prioritize sustainability and minimize negative impacts on the environment. In this chapter, we will explore the principles and techniques involved in managing pests and diseases organically, focusing on natural methods to promote healthy ecosystems and resilient crops.

**Understanding Pest and Disease Management**

Pest and disease management involves a combination of preventive measures and interventions to control populations and limit the damage caused to crops. Organic pest and disease management take a holistic approach, recognizing that the health of the overall ecosystem plays a crucial role in mitigating infestations. Instead of relying solely on chemical solutions, organic farmers look to prevent and manage pests and diseases by promoting biodiversity, improving soil health, and implementing cultural and biological control methods.

**Promoting Biodiversity**

Biodiversity is the key to a healthy and resilient ecosystem. Organic farmers understand the importance of maintaining a diverse range of plants, insects, and animals within their agricultural landscapes. By creating diverse habitats, such as hedgerows, grasslands, and ponds, farmers can encourage a variety of beneficial organisms that act as natural enemies to pests.

Some beneficial organisms, known as predators, prey on and control pest populations. Ladybugs, lacewings, and predatory mites, for example, feed on aphids and other pests. By including flowering plants in their fields, organic farmers attract these predators and provide them with nectar and pollen, ensuring their survival and reproduction.

Another way organic farmers promote biodiversity is by creating nesting sites for beneficial insects. Installing insect hotels or leaving dead wood and plant debris in designated areas allows beneficial bugs, such as ground beetles and parasitoid wasps, to find shelter and reproduce, increasing their presence in the field.

**Improving Soil Health**

Healthy soil is the foundation of any successful organic farm. By focusing on soil health, farmers can enhance the resilience of their crops and reduce their susceptibility to pests and diseases. Soil management practices, such as crop rotation and cover cropping, promote long-term soil health and fertility.

Crop rotation involves alternating the types of crops grown in specific areas seasonally or yearly. This practice disrupts pest life cycles, making it harder for them to establish populations. Additionally, different crops have different nutrient requirements, reducing the buildup of specific pests and diseases. Cover cropping involves growing temporary vegetative cover between cash crops. These cover crops add organic matter to the soil, increase microbial activity, and enhance nutrient cycling, creating a healthier growing environment.

Companion planting is another strategy that combines different plant species within the same area to enhance pest control. Some plants release natural substances that repel pests, while others act as trap crops, attracting pests away from the main crop. For example, planting marigolds around tomato plants can deter aphids, while planting beans close to corn can reduce populations of corn earworms.

**Cultural and Biological Control Methods**

Organic farmers employ cultural methods to manage pests and diseases by manipulating the growing environment to reduce their impact. These methods include practices such as proper irrigation, weed management, and crop sanitation.

Proper irrigation practices, such as drip irrigation or targeted watering, minimize excess moisture, which can promote the development of certain diseases. Weeds act as hosts for pests and diseases, so managing them through regular weeding and mulching is essential to preventing infestations. Crop sanitation involves removing and destroying infected plant material to prevent the spread of diseases. Prompt removal of diseased plants and proper disposal can halt the transmission to healthy plants.

Biological control methods involve the use of natural enemies and biological agents to suppress pests and diseases. The introduction of beneficial insects, such as predatory beetles or parasitic wasps, can regulate pest populations effectively without the need for synthetic pesticides. Similarly, the use of beneficial microbes, such as Bacillus thuringiensis, israelensis (BTI), can control mosquito larvae without affecting other organisms.

Managing pests and diseases organically is a challenging but rewarding endeavor. By prioritizing biodiversity, improving soil health, and implementing cultural and biological control methods, organic farmers are cultivating sustainable and resilient agricultural systems. These methods not only protect the environment but also contribute to the production of nutritious and high-quality crops. As awareness of the benefits of organic agriculture continues to grow, the adoption and refinement of organic pest and disease management techniques will be crucial in ensuring a secure and sustainable food future.

# Handling Environmental Factors and Abiotic Stress

In the constantly evolving natural world, living organisms are inevitably exposed to various environmental factors that can significantly impact their growth and development. These factors, known as abiotic stressors, include temperature extremes, drought, salinity, high light intensity, and pollution. Plants, in particular, face immense challenges as they are immobile and cannot escape unfavorable conditions. However, through the process of evolution, plants have developed remarkable mechanisms to cope with these stressors. In this chapter, we will explore the fascinating strategies employed by plants to handle environmental factors and abiotic stress, shedding light on their resilience and adaptability.

**Temperature Extremes**

Temperature is a crucial factor that profoundly influences plant development. Excessive heat or cold can disrupt cellular processes and lead to permanent damage. To survive and thrive, plants have developed sophisticated mechanisms to withstand temperature extremes. One such mechanism is thermotolerance, wherein plants increase their heat resistance by adjusting their cellular metabolism. The accumulation of heat-shock proteins helps in maintaining protein integrity under elevated temperatures. Furthermore, plants activate heat-stable enzymes that assist in various metabolic reactions.

On the other hand, during cold spells, plants employ a tactic called cold acclimation to enhance their freezing tolerance. This process involves altering the composition of cell membranes, which ensures the plant's vital structures remain intact even in sub-zero temperatures. Additionally, the accumulation of cryoprotectant molecules like sugars and proline helps prevent the formation of ice crystals in plant cells, reducing the risk of injury.

**Drought Stress**

Drought stress is a persistent challenge faced by plants in both natural and agricultural ecosystems. It occurs when the amount of available water becomes limited, leading to plant water deficits. To combat this stress, plants employ various adaptations at the physiological and anatomical levels. One such adaptation is stomatal closure, which reduces water loss through transpiration. Stomata are small pores on leaves through which water vapor escapes, but when plants sense low water availability, they can actively close their stomata to conserve water.

Plants also develop extensive root systems, allowing them to explore larger soil volumes and access water stored deeper in the soil profile during times of low rainfall. Additionally, certain plants possess specialized structures, such as succulent leaves or water-storing tissues, which enable them to store water for prolonged periods, safeguarding them against drought-induced dehydration.

**Salinity Stress**

Salinity stress, stemming from excessive salt accumulation in the soil, poses significant challenges for plant growth. High salt concentrations disrupt the osmotic balance of plant cells, leading to water deprivation and adversely affecting metabolic processes. However, some plants have evolved mechanisms to mitigate the harmful impact of salinity. They employ a process called ion exclusion, wherein they selectively restrict the uptake of toxic ions, such as sodium, from the soil. This prevents sodium accumulation, ensuring the maintenance of optimal cellular osmotic balance.

Furthermore, salt-tolerant plants activate mechanisms to compartmentalize sodium ions within vacuoles, minimizing their negative effects on cellular processes. Some halophytes, plants that naturally grow in high-salt environments, employ specialized salt glands to excrete excess salt from their tissues, enabling them to thrive in highly saline areas.

**High Light Intensity**

While light is essential for photosynthesis, excessive light exposure can lead to photooxidative damage. The high-energy photons absorbed by pigments can generate reactive oxygen species (ROS), which can harm cellular components and disrupt cellular processes. To prevent such damage, plants have developed a range of protective mechanisms.

One of these mechanisms involves the synthesis and accumulation of antioxidant enzymes such as superoxide dismutase, catalase, and peroxidase. These enzymes scavenge ROS, neutralizing their damaging effects on cellular components. Additionally, plants produce specific photoprotective pigments, such as carotenoids, which can dissipate excess light energy as heat and prevent the formation of harmful ROS. Furthermore, some plants adjust their leaf orientation to minimize light exposure, reducing the risk of photooxidative damage.

**Pollution Stress**

With the rapid industrialization and urbanization of our world, pollution poses a growing threat to plant life. Airborne pollutants, including heavy metals, ozone, sulfur dioxide, and nitrogen dioxide, can cause irreparable damage to plant tissues and negatively impact plant growth and development. However, plants exhibit a remarkable ability to tolerate and detoxify these pollutants.

Plants possess a variety of enzymes that detoxify and transform harmful pollutants into less toxic compounds through a process known as phytoremediation. Additionally, certain plants possess specialized structures, such as trichomes or waxy cuticles, that can reduce the absorption of pollutants from the atmosphere. Moreover, plants in polluted areas can undergo epigenetic adaptations, altering their gene expression patterns to cope with the changing environmental conditions.

# Chapter 6: Seasonal Considerations and Crop Rotation

In the world of agriculture, successful farmers understand the crucial significance of seasonal considerations and crop rotation in ensuring the long-term health and productivity of their land. Seasonal changes have a profound impact on the growth patterns of crops, while crop rotation helps to maintain the fertility of the soil, manage pests and diseases, and maximize yields. In this chapter, we will explore the importance of seasonal considerations, delve into the intricacies of crop rotation, and discuss its undeniable benefits for sustainable farming practices.

**Understanding Seasonal Considerations:**

Seasonal considerations in agriculture pertain to the careful observation and understanding of the cyclic changes that occur throughout the year. These changes affect various aspects of crop growth, including temperature, precipitation, daylight duration, and humidity. By aligning our farming practices with these seasonal changes, we can optimize crop growth and minimize losses caused by unfavorable weather conditions.

Temperature plays a fundamental role in determining the

appropriate time for planting and harvesting different crops. Some crops, such as corn and tomatoes, thrive in warmer temperatures, while others, like lettuce and peas, prefer cooler conditions. By understanding these temperature preferences and the average temperature ranges in different seasons, farmers can plan their planting schedules accordingly. Additionally, temperature fluctuations can impact flowering and pollination processes, affecting fruit set and yield. Thus, farmers must take these variations into account when managing their crops.

Precipitation levels and distribution throughout the year are another critical factor for crop growth. While some crops require frequent watering, others can tolerate drier conditions. Farmers must adapt their irrigation practices to deliver the right amount of water based on seasonal rainfall patterns or use efficient irrigation techniques to avoid water scarcity or excess, both of which can negatively impact crop productivity.

Daylight duration is a crucial seasonal consideration for most crops. Plants typically require a certain amount of sunlight to photosynthesize and produce sugars vital for growth. As the days shorten during winter, certain crops enter dormancy or require supplemental lighting to compensate for the reduced daylight duration. Furthermore, variations in daylight can also trigger flowering, seed germination, and other critical growth stages. By understanding these patterns, farmers can optimize planting schedules and light management techniques for particular crops.

Humidity levels significantly influence crop health, affecting both growth and the likelihood of diseases. High humidity and excess moisture can lead to fungal and bacterial diseases, while dry conditions may cause physiological stress and reduce yields. Different crops have varying tolerances to humidity levels, which farmers need to consider when selecting their crops and implementing suitable disease management strategies.

**Crop Rotation: The Key to Sustainable Farming:**
Crop rotation is an age-old agricultural practice that involves intentionally shifting the cultivation of different crops within a given area over multiple growing seasons. This method aims to prevent the depletion of soil nutrients, reduce pest and disease pressures, and improve overall soil health.

Maintaining soil fertility is one of the primary goals of implementing crop rotation. Each crop has its specific nutrient requirements, and continuous cultivation of the same crop in a field can deplete the soil of those nutrients. By rotating crops, farmers ensure that different crops with varying nutrient demands are grown throughout the years, allowing the soil to naturally replenish specific nutrients. For example, leguminous crops, such as beans or clover, have the unique ability to fix atmospheric nitrogen into a usable form for plants. Integrating legumes into crop rotations helps increase soil nitrogen levels, benefiting subsequent crops that require this nutrient.

Crop rotation also aids in managing pests and diseases. Certain pests and pathogens exhibit host specificity, meaning they thrive on particular crops and struggle to survive in the absence of their preferred hosts. By shifting crops, farmers disrupt pest life cycles and reduce the risk of severe infestations. Additionally, some crops, like marigolds and mustard greens, have natural pest-repellent properties. Including these crops in rotation can act as a natural pest control measure, minimizing the dependence on chemicals.

Another advantage of crop rotation is weed management. Different crops suppress and compete with weeds in various ways. By alternating crops with different growth habits, farmers can disrupt weed growth cycles and reduce the overall weed population in a field. This, in turn, diminishes the need for herbicide application, promoting a more environmentally friendly approach to weed control.

Additionally, crop rotation contributes to soil health and structure. Different crops have varying root structures, promoting diverse root networks within the soil. This diversity improves soil aggregation, which enhances rainwater infiltration, reduces erosion, and increases overall soil fertility. Moreover, crop rotation practices that include cover crops, such as rye or buckwheat, help prevent soil erosion, suppress weeds, and add organic matter to enrich the soil.

In this chapter, we have explored the intricacies of seasonal considerations and crop rotation in sustainable farming practices. By attentively observing seasonal changes and aligning farming practices accordingly, farmers can optimize crop growth, minimize losses, and foster agricultural sustainability. Furthermore, implementing crop rotation fosters soil fertility, pest and disease management, weed control, and overall soil health. These practices showcase the indispensable role of environmentally conscious and scientifically informed decisions in modern agricultural systems.

# The Importance of Crop Rotation

In the world of agriculture, one method that has been practiced for centuries and has proven its effectiveness is crop rotation. Crop rotation is a fundamental concept that involves systematically changing the type of crops grown in a specific area over a period of time. This practice aims to enhance soil fertility, control pests and diseases, increase crop yield, and promote sustainable farming practices. In this chapter, we will explore the importance of crop rotation, its historical significance, and its implementation in modern agriculture.

## 1. Historical Significance:

### 1.1 Origins in Ancient Agricultural Societies:

The practice of crop rotation dates back to ancient agricultural civilizations, including the Egyptians, Greeks, and Romans. These civilizations recognized the importance of nurturing and improving the fertility of the soil, which laid the foundation for successful crops and bountiful harvests. They observed that continuously growing the same crop in the same field led to soil depletion, reduced yields, and increased susceptibility to pests and diseases. Consequently, they began experimenting with crop rotation to replenish the soil and achieve sustainable agriculture.

**1.2 Crop Rotation in the Middle Ages:**

During the Middle Ages, the concept of crop rotation continued to evolve. The three-field system, a popular method of crop rotation, was developed in Europe. It divided fields into three sections: one for winter crops, like winter wheat or rye; one for spring crops, such as peas or legumes; and finally, one left fallow to allow the soil to rest and regenerate. This approach was revolutionary as it significantly increased agricultural productivity and sustained the growing population.

**2. Understanding the Science behind Crop Rotation:**

**2.1 Soil Enrichment and Nutrient Cycling:**

One of the primary benefits of crop rotation is the restoration and improvement of soil fertility. Different crops have varying nutrient requirements, and by rotating them, farmers can ensure that each crop utilizes different nutrients, preventing depletion of any single element from the soil. For example, legume crops, such as peas and beans, have the ability to fix nitrogen from the atmosphere and convert it into a form that is available to other plants. By including legumes in a crop rotation plan, farmers can replenish nitrogen levels in the soil, reducing the need for synthetic fertilizers, and minimizing environmental impacts.

## 2.2 Pest and Disease Management:

Crop rotation is an effective strategy to manage pests and diseases in agricultural systems. Many pests and diseases are crop-specific, meaning they rely on specific crops for their survival and reproduction. By rotating crops, farmers disrupt the lifecycle of these pests and create unfavorable conditions for their development. Additionally, pests that primarily target one crop may not find their preferred host in a field where a different crop is grown, resulting in reduced pest populations. Furthermore, crop rotation reduces the build-up of pests and diseases in the soil, as rotating crops disrupts the continuous presence of specific pathogens or insects.

## 3. Enhanced Crop Yield and Quality:

By implementing crop rotation, farmers can significantly improve crop yields and overall quality. Different crops have individual growth requirements, root structures, and nutrient uptake abilities. By alternating crops, farmers ensure that crops do not deplete specific nutrients or accumulate excess elements, which can hinder growth. This enhances the stability and health of the entire crop rotation system, resulting in improved yields and higher-quality produce.

## 4. Environmental Sustainability:

### 4.1 Soil Erosion Control:

Crop rotation plays a crucial role in preventing soil erosion. Growing crops with diverse root structures, such as deep-rooted crops like maize or shallow-rooted ones like clover, creates a more stable soil structure. Deep-rooted crops help loosen compacted soil and improve water infiltration rates, thereby reducing the risk of erosion. Additionally, crop residues left after harvest act as natural ground cover, protecting the soil from wind and water erosion.

### 4.2 Water Management and Conservation:

Crop rotation can aid in water management and conservation. Different crops have varying water requirements, enabling farmers to optimize water usage. For instance, crops with high water requirements, such as rice, can be followed by drought-tolerant crops, like millet or sorghum. This helps balance water usage and reduces the strain on limited water resources, making agriculture more sustainable and resilient in dry regions.

## 5. Modern Crop Rotation Practices:

### 5.1 Integration of Cover Crops:

In modern agricultural systems, cover crops have gained significant importance in crop rotation strategies. Cover crops are noncommercial crops that are grown primarily to improve soil health and protect against erosion. They are an essential component of sustainable agriculture, as they prevent nutrient runoff, suppress weeds, and build soil organic matter. Common cover crops include legumes, grasses, and brassicas, which can be integrated into crop rotation plans to achieve various benefits.

## 5.2 Precision Agriculture and Technology Integration:

Advancements in precision agriculture and technology have revolutionized the implementation of crop rotation. Tools like satellite imagery, drones, and soil sensors provide farmers with valuable information regarding soil fertility, pest presence, and crop performance. By utilizing this data, farmers can make informed decisions about planning crop rotations, choosing suitable crops for specific fields, and adapting their practices to optimize yields while minimizing environmental impacts.

Crop rotation has stood the test of time, from ancient civilizations to modern farming techniques. Its importance cannot be overstated, as it serves as a sustainable solution for maintaining soil health, managing pests and diseases, increasing crop yield, and overall environmental preservation. By continuously evolving and integrating innovative practices and technologies, crop rotation will continue to be a vital component of successful agricultural systems, ensuring the availability of nutritious food for future generations while safeguarding our precious natural resources.

# Planning Successive Plantings

In the world of gardening, planning successive plantings is a crucial aspect that often goes unnoticed by many novice gardeners. Successive plantings involve strategically growing and harvesting crops in a series of sequential plantings to ensure a continuous supply of produce throughout the growing season. This technique not only maximizes the productivity of your garden but also provides a steady stream of fresh fruits, vegetables, and herbs. In this chapter, we will delve into the art of planning successive plantings, discussing the various benefits, techniques, and considerations that will help you achieve a thriving and bountiful garden all year round.

**Understanding the Benefits:**

Planning successive plantings offers several benefits that make it an indispensable technique for gardeners, whether they have modest backyard plots or large-scale agricultural operations.

**1. Extended Harvest Window:**

By staggering the planting of various crops, gardeners can extend their harvest window. Instead of a single crop of tomatoes ripe for picking all at once and then nothing until the next season, successive plantings ensure a continual yield throughout the growing season. This broader harvest window not only allows for a steady supply of fresh produce but also reduces waste as excess crops can be preserved or shared with friends and neighbors.

## 2. Enhanced Crop Rotation:

Crop rotation is vital in maintaining a balanced and healthy garden ecosystem. Planning successive plantings goes hand in hand with effective crop rotation as it allows for the rotation of crops at different stages of growth. This practice helps to prevent soil depletion, disease, and pest buildup, ensuring the long-term success and productivity of your garden.

## 3. Increased Productivity:

Successive plantings significantly increase overall garden productivity. By planting new crops as others are harvested, you can utilize available space more efficiently. This approach eliminates any downtime in your garden and maximizes its yield potential. With careful planning, you can even cultivate multiple crops within the same area in a single growing season, boosting productivity exponentially.

## 4. Season Extension:

Planning successive plantings can help extend the growing season, even in regions with shorter summers or harsh winters. By selecting appropriate crops and utilizing techniques such as row covers, greenhouses, or cold frames, gardeners can continue growing well beyond the expected season. This extended production period offers a wealth of opportunities for cultivating diverse crops, experimenting with different varieties, and pushing the boundaries of what can be grown in your region.

**Strategic Techniques:**

To implement successful successive plantings, it is crucial to optimize your garden layout and select appropriate crops. Here are a few techniques to consider:

## 1. Crop Selection:

Choosing the right crops for successive plantings is key to ensuring a consistent harvest. Determine which crops grow best in your region and align the planting schedule accordingly. Some vegetables, such as lettuce, radishes, spinach, and beets, have quick maturation times. These are excellent choices for successive plantings as they can be sown multiple times throughout the growing season. Conversely, crops like potatoes and winter squash have longer maturation times, making them unsuitable for successive planting unless you have an extended growing season.

## 2. Maturity Dates:

Understanding each crop's average maturity date is essential for planning successive plantings. This knowledge enables you to stagger seed sowings or transplanting dates effectively. By calculating the time it takes for a crop to reach maturity from the sowing date, you can estimate when to plant the subsequent crop. Be sure to account for any variations due to weather, temperature, and specific varieties.

## 3. Succession Planting Techniques:

There are several techniques for succession planting, such as relay and interplanting. Relay planting involves sowing a new crop a fixed interval after the previous one, allowing for a continuous harvest. For example, if you have a row of lettuce plants, you can plant new seedlings every two weeks. As the first row nears maturity and is harvested, the subsequent rows will be ready for harvest soon.

Interplanting, on the other hand, involves growing different crops together simultaneously, with staggered planting dates. This allows you to make maximum use of limited space and ensures a constant supply of produce. For example, you can plant fast-maturing crops, like radishes or green onions, between slower-growing crops like tomatoes or peppers. As the faster crops are harvested, the slower crops have more space to grow.

## 4. Utilizing Successive Seasons:

In addition to planning successive plantings within a single growing season, you can also utilize successive seasons to prolong your harvest. For instance, by planting cool-season crops such as carrots and peas in early spring, you can then follow up with warm-season crops like tomatoes and peppers in late spring or early summer. Once these crops are harvested, you can reintroduce cool-season crops in the fall for an extended growing season.

## Considerations and Challenges:

While planning successive plantings can be highly rewarding, it also presents unique challenges. Here are a few important considerations to keep in mind:

**1. Soil Fertility and Nutrient Management:**

Successive plantings can lead to nutrient depletion, especially if the same crop is grown repeatedly. Implementing proper soil fertility management, such as regular fertilization, adding organic matter, or using cover crops, is crucial in maintaining soil health over time. Crop rotation, as previously mentioned, also helps balance nutrient uptake and minimize the risk of disease and pest infestation.

**2. Pest and Disease Management:**

Intensive planting practices associated with successive plantings can lead to increased susceptibility to pests and diseases. Regular scouting, timely interventions, and good cultural practices, such as proper spacing and adequate airflow, are essential for pest and disease management. Additionally, implementing companion planting techniques that harness the power of beneficial plant relationships can be helpful in deterring pests and promoting plant health.

**3. Watering and Irrigation:**

As you plan successive plantings, it's important to ensure adequate water availability for all crops. Different plants have varying water requirements at different stages of growth. Implementing efficient irrigation systems like drip irrigation or soaker hoses can help maintain consistent moisture levels and prevent water stress. Additionally, mulching can aid in water retention and weed suppression, further optimizing your garden's irrigation needs.

**4. Record Keeping:**

Keeping detailed records of your successive plantings is invaluable for future reference and planning. Maintain a gardening journal or spreadsheet, noting the crop varieties, planting dates, sowing or transplanting techniques, and any observations regarding crop performance, disease incidences, or yield quantities. These records will serve as a valuable resource for fine-tuning your successive planting strategies in subsequent years.

The art of planning successive plantings is a valuable skill for any gardener seeking to maximize their garden's potential. From extending the harvest window to increasing productivity and overcoming seasonal limitations, this technique offers a multitude of benefits. With careful consideration of crop selection, maturity dates, planting techniques, and other important factors, you can create a thriving and abundant garden that yields fresh produce throughout the growing season.

The strategic planning and execution involved in successive plantings will transform your garden into a year-round oasis of flavors and colors, nurturing not only your plants but also your gardening skills.

# Maximizing Year-Round Garden Productivity

In a world where sustainable living and self-sufficiency are gaining increasing importance, having a year-round productive garden is a dream for many individuals. The ability to grow fresh fruits, vegetables, and herbs throughout the year not only saves money but also provides a sense of accomplishment and satisfaction. However, achieving year-round garden productivity requires careful planning, strategic planting, and diligent maintenance. In this chapter, we will explore various techniques and practices that can help you maximize your garden's productivity, regardless of the season.

**Understanding the Seasons**

Before delving into the strategies for year-round garden productivity, it is vital to understand the different seasons and their impact on plant growth. Each season brings unique challenges and opportunities, and tailoring your gardening practices accordingly will greatly enhance your chances of success.

Spring: Spring signifies new beginnings, with longer days and warmer temperatures. In this season, plants awaken from dormancy and rapidly grow. Soil preparation, sowing seeds, and transplanting seedlings are crucial activities during this time. Properly tending to your garden in spring will set the stage for an abundant harvest throughout the year.

Summer: The hot and sunny days of summer pose challenges for gardeners, as dehydration and heat stress can negatively impact plant growth. Adequate watering and mulching are essential to retain moisture in the soil. Furthermore, timely harvesting is crucial to prevent wilting and encourage the continuous production of crops.

Autumn: As temperatures begin to drop, autumn provides a second chance for gardening enthusiasts to prepare for the upcoming winter and ensure a bountiful harvest. Sowing cool-season crops like broccoli, carrots, and spinach allow you to extend your harvest well into the colder months. Additionally, preserving the excess produce through canning, pickling, or freezing will ensure a fresh supply of homegrown goodness throughout winter.

Winter: In regions with harsh winters, gardening efforts may seem futile. However, with the right techniques, it is still possible to enjoy a productive garden during this period. Cold frames, greenhouses, and indoor gardening are some solutions to combat the challenging weather conditions and continue growing fresh produce year-round.

**Selecting Cold-Hardy Plants**

To maximize year-round garden productivity, it is essential to select plant varieties that can withstand cold temperatures. Many plants, such as kale, Brussels sprouts, and collard greens, are resilient to frost and can thrive even in chilly conditions. Additionally, cold-hardy herbs like parsley, thyme, and chives can be grown in containers indoors during winter. By carefully choosing the plant varieties, you can ensure a continuous supply of nutritious greens and flavorful herbs throughout the year.

## Utilizing Season Extenders

To protect your plants from adverse weather conditions and extend the growing season, season extenders are invaluable tools. Cold frames, row covers, hoop houses, and greenhouses are some effective options that help create a microclimate for your plants. These structures act as insulators, trapping heat and preventing frost damage. By utilizing season extenders, you can start planting earlier in spring and continue harvesting later into the fall, greatly increasing your garden's productivity.

## Crop Rotation

Crop rotation is a well-established technique employed by gardeners to prevent soil-borne diseases, eradicate pests, and maintain soil fertility. By rotating crops annually, you reduce the risk of pest or disease build-up and optimize nutrient utilization. Dividing your garden into different sections and rotating plant families each year ensures that the same type of crop is not grown in the same area until after three to four years. This practice improves soil structure, minimizes the need for pesticides, and maximizes overall garden productivity.

**Intercropping and Succession Planting**

Intercropping involves planting multiple crops with different maturity rates in the same area, simultaneously. By doing so, you can effectively maximize space and obtain higher yields from your garden. For example, tall crops like maize or pole beans can provide shade to leafy greens or lettuces growing beneath them. Additionally, succession planting allows you to continually plant new seeds or seedlings to replace harvested crops promptly. This ensures a continuous supply of fresh produce throughout the growing season, optimizing productivity and minimizing any downtime in the garden.

**Companion Planting**

Companion planting is a method of strategically placing certain plants together to achieve mutual benefits. Some plants, when grown together, can repel pests, attract beneficial insects, or enhance nutrient absorption. For instance, planting marigolds alongside tomatoes deters harmful nematodes, while attracting pollinators like bees and butterflies. Similarly, interplanting fragrant herbs like rosemary or basil with vegetables can mask their scent, reducing the risk of insect infestations. By implementing companion planting techniques, you can create a harmonious garden ecosystem that promotes optimal growth and enhances productivity.

**Organic Pest Control**

Pests can wreak havoc on a garden and significantly reduce productivity. Rather than resorting to chemical pesticides, adopting organic pest control methods is not only environmentally friendly but also promotes a healthier ecosystem in your garden.

Encouraging beneficial insects like ladybugs, lacewings, and praying mantises, creates a natural balance and keeps pest populations in check. Additionally, employing physical barriers like netting or traps, handpicking pests, or making homemade organic sprays from garlic or neem oil are effective approaches to preventing pest damage and maximizing yields.

**Soil Health and Fertilization**

The foundation of a productive garden lies in healthy soil. Regularly testing the soil's composition and pH level allows you to amend it accordingly to optimize plant growth. Adding organic matter in the form of compost, well-rotted manure, or leaf mulch helps improve soil structure, retain moisture, and enhance nutrient availability. Furthermore, practicing cover cropping during fallow periods helps prevent soil erosion, promotes organic matter accumulation, and suppresses weed growth. By nurturing your soil, you create an ideal environment for your plants to thrive and maximize their productivity.

As an avid gardener, your journey to year-round garden productivity requires careful planning, dedication, and continuous learning. The strategies discussed in this chapter, including understanding the seasons, selecting cold-hardy plants, utilizing season extenders, crop rotation, intercropping, companion planting, organic pest control, and nurturing soil health, will set you on the right path to achieving your garden goals. Remember, gardening is a lifelong pursuit, and as you gain knowledge and experience, the rewards of a productive and self-sustaining garden will continue to grow along with it.

# Chapter 7: Sustainable Practices for an Eco-Friendly Garden

In today's world, the importance of protecting the environment and embracing sustainability has become paramount. As gardeners, we have a unique opportunity to make meaningful contributions to creating a healthier planet. By adopting sustainable practices in our gardens, we can minimize the negative impact on our ecosystems while still enjoying beautiful and flourishing spaces. In this chapter, we will explore several eco-friendly techniques and approaches that will empower you to create a sustainable garden that thrives in harmony with nature.

**1. Planning and Designing with Sustainability in Mind:**

Building a sustainable garden starts with careful planning and design. Before you begin planting, take the time to analyze your garden site and consider factors such as sunlight exposure, soil conditions, and water availability. By understanding these elements, you can optimize your garden's potential while minimizing resource consumption.

**Consider implementing the following sustainable design principles:**

a) Native Planting: Choose native plants that are adapted to your region's climate and require minimal maintenance. Indigenous species provide habitat and food for local wildlife, support biodiversity, and reduce the need for excessive watering and fertilization.

b) Diverse Plant Selection: Create a diverse plant community with different types of flora. This approach promotes natural pest control, enhances resilience against diseases, and minimizes the need for chemical interventions.

c) Efficient Watering Techniques: Install a smart irrigation system or use drip irrigation to ensure water efficiency. Additionally, group plants with similar water requirements, so you can irrigate them appropriately without wasting resources.

d) Composting: Integrate composting into your garden plans. Composting not only reduces waste but also produces nutrient-rich soil amendments, providing a sustainable source of healthy nourishment for your plants.

**2. Soil Health and Fertility:**

Maintaining healthy soil is essential for a resilient and eco-friendly garden. Healthy soil supports plant growth, retains moisture, and reduces erosion. By adopting sustainable practices, you can improve soil health and minimize the need for synthetic fertilizers and harmful chemicals.

**Consider the following sustainable soil practices:**

a) Mulching: Mulching helps retain soil moisture, suppresses weed growth, and improves soil structure. Use organic mulch such as wood chips, straw, or shredded leaves to encourage decomposition and enrich the soil with organic matter over time.

b) Cover Cropping: Integrate cover crops into your garden rotation plans. Cover crops, such as legumes or grasses, prevent soil erosion, increase nutrient availability, and control pests naturally. When these crops are tilled or mowed, they become a green manure that adds nutrients back into the soil.

c) Vermicomposting: Start a worm composting system in your garden to recycle kitchen scraps and produce nutrient-rich worm castings. Vermicompost enhances soil fertility, improves water-holding capacity, and reduces the need for synthetic fertilizers.

d) Avoid Over-Tilling: Excessive tilling disrupts the soil structure, leading to erosion and loss of beneficial microorganisms. Employ no-till or reduced-till methods to maintain soil health and conserve energy.

## 3. Responsible Pest and Weed Management:

Dealing with pests and weeds can be a challenge for any gardener. However, by employing sustainable practices, you can manage these issues while minimizing the use of harmful chemicals that harm beneficial insects, pollinators, and the environment.

Consider implementing these eco-friendly pest and weed management strategies:

a) Integrated Pest Management (IPM): Employ an IPM approach that combines a range of control methods. IPM includes strategies such as biological controls (introducing predators or parasites), mechanical controls (hand-picking pests), and cultural controls (companion planting or crop rotation) before considering targeted, low-toxicity pesticides.

b) Beneficial Insects: Attract beneficial insects to your garden by planting flowers that provide nectar and pollen. Ladybugs, lacewings, and parasitic wasps are excellent natural predators that combat common pests like aphids and caterpillars.

c) Weed Control: Regularly weed your garden by hand or use mulch to suppress weed growth. Avoid using chemical herbicides that can harm beneficial plants, contaminate water sources, and have long-lasting effects on the environment.

d) Companion Planting: Utilize companion planting, where certain plants are grown together to repel pests, attract beneficial insects, or improve overall plant health. For example, marigolds deter nematodes, while basil repels mosquitoes and aphids.

## 4. Water Conservation:

In regions where water is scarce, practicing water conservation in the garden is crucial for sustainability. Even if you have ample water resources, minimizing water waste should always be a priority.

**Consider the following strategies for conserving water:**

a) Rainwater Harvesting: Install rain barrels or storage tanks to collect rainwater for irrigation purposes. Diverting water from your roof into barrels will reduce runoff, cut down on your water bill, and provide a chlorine-free water source for your plants.

b) Xeriscaping: Embrace xeriscaping techniques, particularly in arid regions, by choosing native or drought-tolerant plants that require less water. Use efficient irrigation methods such as drip irrigation or soaker hoses to deliver water directly to the plants' roots.

c) Mulching: As mentioned earlier, mulching plays a vital role in conserving water by reducing evaporation. Apply a generous layer of organic mulch around your plants to retain soil moisture and minimize the need for frequent watering.

d) Timing and Frequency: Water your garden early in the morning or late in the evening when temperatures are cooler, reducing water loss due to evaporation. Additionally, water deeply but less frequently to encourage plants to develop deeper root systems, making them more resilient during dry periods.

# Embracing Organic Gardening Methods

In today's fast-paced world, there is a growing awareness of the impact of our actions on the environment. As more people become conscious of their environmental footprint, a movement towards organic gardening has gained momentum. Organic gardening is a natural, sustainable approach to cultivating plants that emphasizes the use of natural materials and practices, while reducing reliance on harmful chemicals and synthetic products. In this chapter, we will explore the principles, techniques, and benefits of organic gardening, providing you with the knowledge and tools to embrace this eco-friendly method.

**Understanding Organic Gardening:**

Organic gardening goes beyond simply avoiding the use of chemicals and synthetic fertilizers. It is a holistic approach that focuses on nourishing the soil, promoting biodiversity, and fostering a harmonious relationship between plants, animals, and humans. By working with nature rather than against it, organic gardening aims to create healthy, resilient ecosystems that support plant growth and the overall wellbeing of the environment.

**Building Healthy Soil:**

The foundation of successful organic gardening lies in nurturing healthy soil. Unlike conventional gardening, which often relies on chemical fertilizers, organic gardening employs organic matter to improve soil structure and fertility. Compost, comprised of decomposed organic materials like kitchen scraps, leaves, and grass clippings, is a key component in organic soil enrichment. Adding compost to your garden beds boosts soil fertility, enhances moisture retention, and promotes beneficial microbial activity, resulting in luscious and bountiful plant growth.

**Controlling Weeds Naturally:**

In traditional gardening, chemical herbicides are commonly used to eradicate weeds. However, organic gardening offers various natural methods to control weeds without harming the environment. One popular technique is mulching, which involves covering the soil surface with organic materials such as straw, wood chips, or shredded leaves. Mulch acts as a barrier, preventing weed growth by blocking sunlight and suffocating unwanted plants. Additionally, hand-weeding and regular cultivation using a garden fork or hoe help keep weeds at bay, while maintaining a healthy ecosystem.

**Pest and Disease Management:**

Managing pests and diseases is a significant challenge for any gardener, but organic gardeners approach this issue in an environmentally friendly manner. Rather than relying on synthetic pesticides, organic gardening focuses on prevention, encouraging natural predators to keep pest populations in check. Practices such as intercropping, companion planting, and creating insectary borders help attract beneficial insects which prey upon garden pests. Furthermore, using homemade organic sprays made from ingredients such as garlic, neem oil, or soap can effectively control certain pests without harming beneficial insects or the broader ecosystem.

## Encouraging Biodiversity:

One of the core principles of organic gardening is promoting biodiversity. By cultivating a diverse range of plants, you attract a variety of beneficial organisms, including insects, birds, and microorganisms, which play critical roles in maintaining a balanced ecosystem. In addition to attracting beneficial insects with flowering plants, you can also create wildlife-friendly habitats by incorporating birdhouses, bat boxes, and ponds into your garden design. Embracing biodiversity enhances the resilience of your garden, increases pollination rates, and helps control pests naturally.

## Sustainable Water Usage:

In a world increasingly facing water scarcity, it is essential to adopt sustainable water management practices in gardening. Organic gardening embraces techniques that focus on water conservation and efficient usage. Mulching plays a vital role in regulating soil moisture, reducing evaporation, and minimizing the need for frequent watering. Furthermore, utilizing drip irrigation systems or installing rainwater harvesting systems can help capture and reuse rainwater, reducing dependence on municipal water supplies and promoting responsible water usage.

## The Benefits of Organic Gardening:

Embracing organic gardening extends numerous benefits beyond environmental sustainability. By growing organic produce, you prioritize your health and the wellbeing of those consuming the food you cultivate. Organic crops are free from synthetic chemicals, pesticides, and genetically modified organisms, ensuring that you provide your family with fresh and nutritious food that is free from potentially harmful substances.

Organic gardening also grants you an opportunity to connect with nature and enjoy a peaceful and rewarding hobby. Gardening has been shown to reduce stress levels, improve mental wellbeing, and foster a sense of fulfillment. Moreover, engaging in organic gardening allows you to contribute to the resilience and conservation of valuable ecosystems, protecting biodiversity and preserving the planet for future generations.

In this chapter, we have dived into the world of organic gardening, exploring its principles, techniques, and benefits. We have learned that organic gardening is not just about avoiding harmful chemicals but about embracing a sustainable and holistic approach to nurturing plants, soil, and ecosystems. By adopting methods that prioritize soil health, natural weed control, pest management, biodiversity, and sustainable water usage, we become stewards of the environment and allies of nature. Embracing the art of organic gardening not only contributes to the wellbeing of the planet but also nourishes our physical and mental health, bringing us closer to the natural world and fostering a harmonious relationship with Earth's bountiful resources.

# Composting and Soil Health

In today's world, where concerns about climate change and environmental degradation are growing, it is essential to adopt sustainable practices to ensure the health of our planet. One such practice that has gained significant attention is composting. Composting is a natural process that converts organic waste into nutrient-rich soil amendments, thus promoting soil health and fertility. In this chapter, we will explore the profound relationship between composting and soil health and understand how this ancient practice can address modern-day environmental challenges.

**The Basics of Composting**

Composting is a simple yet fascinating process that harnesses the power of natural decomposition. It involves gathering organic waste materials, such as kitchen scraps, yard trimmings, and manure, and creating the ideal conditions for microorganisms to break them down into nutrient-rich compost. These microorganisms, primarily bacteria, fungi, and earthworms, thrive in an aerobic environment that is well-aerated, moist, and rich in carbon and nitrogen.

To start composting, it is crucial to have a balance of green and brown materials. Green materials, high in nitrogen, provide a source of protein for microorganisms. These include fruit and vegetable scraps, coffee grounds, and fresh grass clippings. Brown materials, high in carbon, act as a source of energy to fuel decomposition.

Examples of brown materials are dry leaves, straw, and shredded newspaper. By combining these materials, we achieve a carbon-to-nitrogen ratio (C:N) that supports microbial activity and ensures efficient composting.

## The Relationship Between Composting and Soil Health

Composting exerts a multitude of positive effects on soil health. Let us explore some of the significant ways in which compost enhances soil fertility, structure, and overall health.

### 1. Nutrient Enrichment:

Compost is a nutrient powerhouse. It provides an abundant supply of essential plant nutrients such as nitrogen, phosphorus, and potassium – the famous NPK trio. Besides these macronutrients, compost also contains trace elements critical for plant growth, including calcium, magnesium, and iron. By amending soils with compost, we replenish nutrient stocks and create an optimal nutrient balance that supports plant growth and productivity.

### 2. Soil Structure Improvement:

The addition of compost enhances soil structure and porosity, contributing to better soil drainage and aeration. The organic matter in compost acts as a sponge, holding moisture in sandy soils and increasing water-holding capacity in clay soils. The improved structure creates a favorable environment for root exploration and penetration, facilitating the uptake of water, nutrients, and oxygen. Moreover, the humus formed during the composting process helps to stabilize soil aggregates, preventing erosion and nutrient leaching.

### 3. Microbial Activity Boost:

Healthy soils are teeming with diverse microbial life, including bacteria, fungi, and other microorganisms. Compost acts as a microbial inoculant, introducing beneficial microbes and stimulating their activity. These microbes help break down organic matter further, release nutrients from organic compounds, and suppress harmful pathogens and pests. By promoting microbial biodiversity and activity, composting significantly contributes to overall soil health.

### 4. pH Regulation:

Soil pH plays a vital role in plant nutrition and microbial activity. Compost has the unique ability to buffer soil pH, preventing extreme swings in acidity or alkalinity. This buffering capacity helps maintain a near-neutral pH, which is ideal for most plants. Furthermore, compost's ability to reduce soil acidity can be particularly beneficial in highly weathered or acid-prone soils.

### 5. Carbon Sequestration:

One of the most compelling benefits of composting is its potential to mitigate climate change by sequestering carbon. Composting ensures that organic waste materials do not end up in landfills, where they decompose anaerobically, releasing methane – a potent greenhouse gas. Instead, composting promotes the conversion of organic matter into stable humus, storing carbon in the soil for prolonged periods. By composting, we contribute to reducing greenhouse gas emissions and combatting climate change.

**Applications and Methods of Composting**

Composting can be applied in various contexts, from small-scale, home composting to large-scale, industrial operations. Let us explore some prevalent composting methods and their applications:

**1. Backyard Composting:**

Backyard composting is the most accessible and widely practiced form of composting. It allows individuals to convert organic waste from their kitchens and gardens into a valuable resource. Common methods include using a compost bin or pile, where materials are layered and turned periodically to ensure decomposition. This method is suitable for small-scale composting and can be easily integrated into home gardening practices.

**2. Vermicomposting:**

Vermicomposting harnesses the unique ability of earthworms to break down organic matter efficiently. This method involves creating a specialized habitat, such as a worm bin, and introducing a specific type of earthworm, typically red wigglers. The worms consume organic waste, leaving behind nutrient-rich castings, also known as vermicompost. Vermicomposting is ideal for individuals with limited outdoor space and is a popular option for indoor composting.

## 3. Windrow Composting:

Windrow composting is a large-scale composting method commonly used in agricultural and municipal operations. It involves piling organic waste in long, narrow rows, known as windrows, and turning them periodically to maintain aeration and temperature. Windrow composting requires more space, machinery, and management compared to backyard composting but can process significant quantities of organic waste efficiently.

## 4. Aerated Static Pile Composting:

This method combines the benefits of windrow composting with better aeration control. It involves creating a large pile of organic waste and incorporating a system of perforated pipes to supply air and regulate temperature. Aerated static pile composting is commonly used in commercial and institutional settings, ensuring faster and more controlled decomposition.

# Water Conservation Techniques

Water is the essence of life, and its conservation is a matter of utmost importance. As the global population continues to grow, the demand for clean water is increasing exponentially. Water scarcity is becoming a severe concern in many parts of the world, leading to devastating consequences for both humans and the environment. To combat this issue, it is crucial to adopt effective water conservation techniques that enable us to make the most of this valuable resource. In this chapter, we will explore various methods and approaches to conserve water, helping us sustainably manage our water resources.

## 1. Efficient Irrigation Systems:

Agricultural practices often account for a significant portion of water usage. An efficient irrigation system can greatly reduce water wastage. Traditional flood irrigation methods, which flood fields with water, have a low efficiency rate and can lead to excessive water loss through evaporation and runoff. However, advanced techniques such as drip irrigation and sprinkler systems have revolutionized the way water is used in agriculture.

Drip irrigation involves delivering water directly to the plant roots, minimizing evaporation and ensuring plants receive precisely the amount of water they need. Sprinkler systems, on the other hand, distribute water over the field using overhead sprinklers, making it an ideal method for certain crops. Implementing such efficient irrigation systems not only conserves water but also promotes healthier crop growth and reduces soil erosion.

## 2. Rainwater Harvesting:

Rainwater harvesting is a centuries-old technique that allows us to collect and utilize rainwater for various purposes. Generally, rainwater is harvested by directing it from rooftops into storage tanks or underground cisterns. This method helps to minimize stormwater runoff and recharge groundwater reserves.

Rainwater harvested from rooftops can be used for non-potable purposes like irrigation, toilet flushing, and washing cars. In arid regions, where water scarcity is a prevailing issue, communities can even treat harvested rainwater to make it safe for drinking. By adopting rainwater harvesting techniques, we can reduce our dependence on freshwater sources and alleviate water stress in water-scarce areas.

## 3. Greywater Recycling:

Greywater refers to wastewater generated from domestic activities such as showering, bathing, and washing dishes, which is not contaminated with fecal matter. Instead of allowing this water to go down the drain and mix with sewage, it can be treated and reused for gardening, toilet flushing, and even laundry.

Greywater recycling systems involve diverting greywater to a separate treatment unit where it undergoes filtration and disinfection processes. Upon treatment, the water can be reused, reducing the overall demand for freshwater. By implementing greywater recycling techniques both at the individual and community level, significant volumes of water can be conserved while concurrently reducing the burden on sewage treatment plants.

## 4. Xeriscaping:

Xeriscaping refers to landscaping techniques that utilize plants and landscaping practices suitable for dry regions, minimizing the need for excessive watering. By selecting native and drought-tolerant plants, creating efficient irrigation systems, using mulch to retain soil moisture, and designing the landscape to prevent water runoff, xeriscaping can significantly reduce outdoor water usage.

Moreover, minimizing the area of lawns, which require large amounts of water to stay green, and replacing them with more water-efficient alternatives such as gravel beds or native plantings helps conserve water. Xeriscaping not only saves water but also reduces the need for chemical fertilizers and pesticides, creating a more sustainable and environmentally friendly outdoor space.

## 5. Proper Plumbing Fixtures:

It is estimated that around 20% of household water usage goes to waste due to leaks and inefficient plumbing fixtures. By adopting water-efficient plumbing fixtures, we can reduce water wastage, save money, and contribute to water conservation efforts.

Installing low-flow showerheads, faucets, and toilets can drastically reduce water consumption without compromising functionality. Low-flow toilets use significantly less water per flush by incorporating technology such as dual flush systems or pressure-assisted mechanisms. Aerators can be added to faucets and showerheads to maintain water pressure while reducing water flow.

**6. Public Awareness and Education:**

Increasing public awareness about the importance of water conservation is vital for long-term changes in water usage patterns. Educational campaigns, workshops, and seminars can effectively inform individuals about water-saving tips and techniques that can be implemented in their daily lives.

Additionally, schools and universities can play a crucial role in educating the younger generation about water conservation. Including water-saving practices as part of the curriculum can create a lasting impact, fostering a culture of responsible water usage from an early age.

**7. Government Policies and Regulations:**

Governments can play a significant role in promoting water conservation by developing policies and regulations that support responsible water usage. Setting water efficiency standards for appliances, implementing water pricing mechanisms that reflect the cost of water scarcity, and providing incentives for water-saving practices can all encourage individuals and businesses to adopt water conservation measures.

Governments can also invest in water infrastructure projects, such as the construction of wastewater treatment plants, rainwater harvesting systems, and desalination plants. These initiatives can help meet the growing water demand while conserving freshwater resources and ensuring their availability for future generations.

Water conservation is a global imperative that requires collective efforts at every level – from individual actions to government policies and industry practices. By implementing and promoting efficient irrigation systems, rainwater harvesting, greywater recycling, xeriscaping, proper plumbing fixtures, public awareness campaigns, and supportive government policies, we can pave the way for a future where water is used sustainably and judiciously.

Remember, every drop counts. Start implementing water conservation techniques today, and together, we can secure a water-rich future for generations to come.

# Attracting Beneficial Wildlife for Pest Control

In the vast realm of nature, balance is the key to survival and growth. Within every ecosystem, there exists a delicate harmony between different organisms. As gardeners, we often find ourselves striving to maintain this balance by managing pests that threaten the health of our plants. However, nature has provided us with a valuable ally in our battle against garden pests: beneficial wildlife. By attracting these creatures to our gardens, we can establish a natural pest control system that minimizes the need for harmful chemicals and fosters a thriving, vibrant environment. In this chapter, we will explore the diverse range of beneficial wildlife and discuss strategies to attract them to our gardens.

## 1. Understanding the Importance of Beneficial Wildlife:

Beneficial wildlife refers to organisms that contribute positively to our gardens by controlling pest populations and promoting ecological balance. Unlike harmful pests that pose a threat to our plants, these creatures have evolved over time to become natural predators or beneficial partners with plants. Attracting beneficial wildlife not only helps manage pest issues but also improves pollination rates, enhances soil health, and increases overall biodiversity - all crucial factors in maintaining a healthy garden ecosystem.

## 2. Birds as Pest Controllers:

### 2.1. Songbirds:

Among the most efficient pest controllers in our gardens are songbirds, which include warblers, sparrows, and finches. These birds feast on a wide range of insects, such as caterpillars, aphids, beetles, and snails, helping to keep their populations in check. To attract songbirds, provide food sources like sunflower seeds and berries, along with sheltered areas like dense shrubs or nest boxes.

### 2.2. Owls and Raptors:

Owls and raptors play a crucial role in controlling rodents and small mammals that can wreak havoc in our gardens. By creating a welcoming habitat with tall trees, nesting platforms, and food sources like mice or voles, we can encourage these majestic birds of prey to take up residence, effectively keeping the rodent population under control.

## 3. Beneficial Insects:

### 3.1. Ladybugs:

Ladybugs, also known as ladybirds or lady beetles, are often regarded as the ultimate garden heroes. These charming little creatures devour aphids, scale insects, mites, and even small caterpillars. To attract ladybugs to your garden, plant nectar-producing flowers like dill, fennel, or yarrow, and provide water sources such as shallow dishes with pebbles.

### 3.2. Lacewings:

Lacewings are nocturnal insects that consume a vast number of soft-bodied pests, including aphids, mealybugs, whiteflies, and thrips. To entice these delicate insects, provide a diverse range of flowering plants like cosmos, coreopsis, and dandelions, which offer a good supply of nectar and pollen as food sources.

## 4. Reptiles and Amphibians:
### 4.1. Snakes:
While snakes may seem intimidating, many of them are beneficial for your garden's ecosystem. Nonvenomous snakes, such as garter snakes and rat snakes, help control the population of rodents like mice and voles that can ravage our crops. Create a habitat suitable for snakes by incorporating features such as rock piles, brush piles, and water sources like small ponds or birdbaths.

### 4.2. Frogs and Toads:
Frogs and toads are voracious eaters of slugs, snails, and many types of insects. Their diet not only reduces the population of these pests but also provides an enjoyable symphony of croaking during summer evenings. Attract frogs and toads by including a water feature such as a small pond, providing shelter in the form of rocks and leaf piles, and minimizing the use of pesticides and herbicides.

## 5. Mammals:
### 5.1. Bats:
Bats are nocturnal creatures that provide a remarkable pest control service by feasting on insects like mosquitoes, moths, and beetles. Attract bats to your garden by installing bat houses, which mimic the natural roosts found in trees, and by planting night-blooming flowers

like evening primrose or moonflower to attract the insects they feed upon.

**5.2. Hedgehogs:**

Hedgehogs are endearing creatures that consume a broad array of garden pests, including slugs, snails, worms, caterpillars, and beetles. By creating hedgehog-friendly spaces with log piles, dense shrubbery, and access to fresh water, you can encourage these spiky allies to make your garden their haven.

**6. Creating a Wildlife-Friendly Garden:**

Creating a garden that attracts beneficial wildlife involves designing a space that provides food, water, shelter, and nesting sites for a wide range of animals. Some general tips include:
- Planting a diverse range of flowers, herbs, and shrubs that provide nectar, pollen, and berries throughout the year.
- Incorporating water features such as birdbaths, ponds, or small pools to provide hydration.
- Limiting the use of pesticides and herbicides, as they can harm both beneficial wildlife and the environment.
- Maintaining a balance between open spaces and dense vegetation to cater to different species' requirements for feeding and shelter.
- Adding nesting boxes, roosting spots, or suitable containers to accommodate the needs of birds, bats, and certain insects.
- Creating habitat patches like rock piles, fallen logs, or leaf litter that offer hiding places for reptiles, amphibians, and small mammals.

# Chapter 8: Scaling Up: Container Gardening and Urban Agriculture

In recent years, there has been a significant shift towards urbanization, with more and more people residing in cities. As the concrete jungles expand, so does the need for creative solutions to sustain the growing population. Thankfully, container gardening and urban agriculture have emerged as effective strategies to address this challenge. In this chapter, we will explore the concept of scaling up these practices, delving into the various aspects that need to be considered to ensure success. From selecting suitable containers and plants to optimizing space and managing resources, this chapter will equip you with the knowledge and inspiration to embark on your own urban gardening journey.

**Section 1: Choosing Suitable Containers:**

Container gardening is the ideal solution for urban environments where space is often limited. Selecting the right containers is crucial for plant health and productivity. When choosing containers, consider factors such as material, size, and drainage. Clay pots are excellent choices as they allow for proper airflow and drainage, preventing root rot. However, they can be heavy and prone to cracking. Plastic containers, on the other hand, are lightweight, affordable, and have better moisture retention. Whichever material you opt for, ensure that the containers are at least 12 inches deep to accommodate root growth adequately.

## Section 2: Selecting Appropriate Plants:

Choosing the right plants for container gardening is essential to maximize productivity and utilize available space efficiently. While almost any plant can be grown in containers, selecting varieties that are well-suited for vertical growth or have compact habits is advisable. Vine plants such as tomatoes, cucumbers, and peas can be trained to grow upward with the help of trellises or stakes, saving valuable horizontal space. Additionally, dwarf varieties of fruit trees and compact herbs are particularly suitable for container gardening, providing both aesthetic appeal and a bountiful harvest.

## Section 3: Space Optimization:

In an urban environment, every square inch counts! Optimizing space is crucial for successful container gardening. Vertical gardening techniques offer an ingenious solution by utilizing walls, fences, and trellises to grow plants upward, reducing the footprint required for a thriving garden. Hanging containers or window boxes can also be utilized to make use of otherwise unused space. Additionally, consider using tiered shelving units or pallets to create multi-level plant displays, further maximizing space.

**Section 4: Managing Resources:**

Proper management of resources is essential to ensure optimal growth and productivity in container gardens. Soil quality, watering, and nutrient supply are all crucial elements. Choosing a high-quality potting mix specifically designed for container gardening is paramount, as it provides adequate drainage and nutrient retention. Organic fertilizers or slow-release fertilizers can be incorporated to fulfill the nutrient requirements of the plants. Additionally, efficient watering techniques, such as using drip irrigation or self-watering containers, can minimize water waste while maintaining soil moisture levels.

**Section 5: Dealing with Challenges:**

Like any form of gardening, container gardening and urban agriculture pose their own set of challenges. Pests, diseases, and environmental factors can potentially harm the plants. To mitigate these risks, implementing integrated pest management strategies like companion planting, crop rotation, and physical barriers can deter pests effectively. Regular monitoring of plants for signs of disease or nutrient deficiencies is crucial, allowing for early intervention to prevent worsening conditions. Furthermore, being aware of local weather patterns and adapting gardening practices accordingly can help manage challenging environmental conditions such as excessive heat or humidity.

**Section 6: Community Engagement and Collaborative Efforts:**

The beauty of container gardening and urban agriculture lies not only in its ability to provide fresh produce but also in its potential to foster community engagement and collaboration. Creating community gardens, rooftop gardens, or shared public spaces can encourage people to come together, share resources, and learn from each other. These collaborative efforts not only promote healthy eating habits but also foster a sense of belonging, improve mental health, and enhance urban aesthetics.

**Section 7: Scaling Up and the Future of Urban Agriculture:**

As container gardening and urban agriculture gain traction, the potential for scaling up these practices becomes more significant. The future of urban agriculture lies in innovative solutions such as vertical farming, aquaponics, and rooftop gardens. These technologies allow for increased productivity in limited spaces, making them particularly attractive for densely populated areas. Furthermore, developments in automation and data-driven farming can optimize resource utilization and improve efficiency, paving the way for a sustainable and resilient urban food system.

# Exploring Container Gardening

Gardening is not limited to those fortunate enough to have a spacious backyard or a dedicated piece of land. With the emergence of container gardening, anyone can become a gardener, regardless of living arrangements or available space. Container gardening offers a flexible and creative way to enjoy the beauty and benefits of nature, even in urban environments or where ground space is limited. In this chapter, we will explore the ins and outs of container gardening, from choosing the right containers to selecting plants and providing adequate care. Let us embark on this exciting journey and discover the captivating world of container gardening.

**Choosing the Right Containers**

Containers are the foundation of any successful container garden. They come in various shapes, sizes, and materials, each with its own set of advantages and considerations. When selecting containers, it is crucial to keep in mind the needs of the plants and the desired aesthetic appeal.

Terracotta pots are classic choices that add a touch of elegance to any garden. Being porous, they allow better airflow for the plants' roots and minimize the risk of overwatering. However, this porous nature also means that terracotta pots dry out faster, requiring more frequent watering. They may also crack in extreme temperatures, so be mindful of the climate in your area.

Plastic containers, on the other hand, are lightweight and non-porous, making them ideal for smaller plants and indoor gardening. They retain water better than terracotta, reducing the frequency of watering. Plastic containers are also less prone to cracking and can withstand various weather conditions, making them versatile options for all kinds of gardens.

Additionally, there are fabric containers, which have gained popularity in recent years. These breathable containers promote healthy root growth by allowing air to reach the plants' roots while preventing them from becoming waterlogged. Fabric pots also enable heat to dissipate quickly, preventing the roots from overheating. These containers are durable, easy to store, and eco-friendly, as they are often made from recycled materials.

Now that we have explored various container options, let us move on to selecting the appropriate plants for your container garden.

## Selecting Plants for Your Container Garden

Choosing the right plants is essential for a thriving container garden. It is crucial to consider factors such as sunlight requirements, plant size, and compatibility when selecting plants. Here are a few guidelines to ensure a harmonious and visually appealing container garden:

1. Consider Sunlight Requirements: Determine the amount of sunlight your desired plants need and assess the available light in your gardening area. Place sun-loving plants, such as tomatoes or zinnias, in containers that receive ample sunlight, while shade-loving plants like ferns or impatiens should be placed in partially shaded areas.

2. Match Plant Size to Container Size: Larger plants require more substantial containers to provide enough space for their roots and prevent them from becoming root-bound. Conversely, smaller plants thrive in smaller containers and can be grouped together for a visually appealing display.

3. Complementing Plants: Consider combining plants with complementary growth habits and similar care requirements. For instance, pairing a tall, upright plant with a trailing one will create a visually appealing arrangement while optimizing the use of space.

4. Thriller, Filler, and Spiller: Implement the "thriller, filler, and spiller" concept when designing your container garden. The thriller is the focal point, usually a tall or eye-catching plant. The fillers are medium-sized plants that add volume and fill the container, while the spillers trail over the edges, softening the container's appearance.

**Caring for Your Container Garden**

Successful container gardening requires proper care and

maintenance. Watering, fertilizing, and ensuring adequate drainage are crucial factors in promoting healthy plant growth. Here are some essential care tips to consider:

1. Watering: Containers tend to dry out faster than traditional garden beds, especially those made of porous materials. Regular watering is vital to prevent the plants from becoming dehydrated. Check the moisture level of the soil regularly and adjust your watering schedule based on the specific needs of your plants.

2. Adequate Drainage: Proper drainage is essential to prevent waterlogging, which can lead to root rot and other plant diseases. Ensure that your containers have drainage holes at the bottom and place saucers or trays to collect excess water while allowing it to drain away.

3. Fertilization: Container plants often require additional fertilization since nutrients in the soil can deplete more rapidly than in ground gardens. Choose a suitable fertilizer specific to your plant's needs and follow the recommended dosage instructions. Regular fertilization will provide the essential nutrients for healthy growth and vibrant blooms.

4. Pruning and Deadheading: Regular pruning promotes bushier growth and prevents plants from becoming leggy. Remove spent flowers, known as deadheading, to encourage further blooming. Pruning and deadheading will help maintain the overall health and appearance of your container garden.

5. Pest and Disease Management: Container gardens are not immune to pests and diseases. Regularly inspect your plants for signs of infestation or disease and take appropriate action. Use organic or chemical treatments to control pests and diseases, depending on your preferred gardening approach.

Container gardening offers a world of possibilities for both experienced and novice gardeners. Its versatility, accessibility, and creative potential make it a popular choice among urban dwellers and those with limited outdoor space. In this chapter, we explored the importance of choosing the right containers, selecting suitable plants, and providing proper care to maintain a thriving container garden. With a little time, effort, and creativity, you can transform any small space into a flourishing oasis. So, grab your containers, select your favorite plants, and embark on a rewarding journey into the captivating world of container gardening.

# Selecting the Right Containers and Soil Mixes

In the world of gardening, the selection of containers and soil mixes plays a pivotal role in the optimal growth and development of plants. Whether you are a seasoned gardener or a beginner, understanding the importance of choosing the right containers and soil mixes is essential to ensure the health and vibrancy of your plants. In this chapter, we will explore the various factors to consider when selecting containers and soil mixes, and provide you with expert tips and recommendations to help you create the perfect environment for your beloved plants.

**Choosing the Right Containers:**

When it comes to selecting containers for your plants, there are a few key factors to consider. Here, we will discuss the different types of containers available and the pros and cons of each:

**1. Plastic Containers:**

Plastic containers are the most widely used type due to their affordability, versatility, and durability. They come in various sizes, colors, and shapes, allowing you to select the perfect one for your plants. On the downside, plastic containers may not provide adequate drainage if they lack drainage holes. It's important to ensure proper drainage to prevent waterlogging, which can lead to root rot.

## 2. Terra Cotta Pots:

Terra cotta pots are classic and aesthetically pleasing, with their natural orange-brown hue. They are known for their breathability, ideal for plants that require good air circulation. However, terra cotta pots tend to dry out quickly, making them more suitable for plants that don't mind dry conditions. Additionally, they are prone to cracking in freezing temperatures.

## 3. Ceramic Pots:

Ceramic pots are known for their decorative appeal and come in a wide range of styles, colors, and textures. These pots are great for indoor plants, adding a touch of elegance to any space. However, they can be heavier than other types of containers, making them less convenient for outdoor use. Ceramic pots also require careful watering, as they do not offer as much breathability as terra cotta pots.

## 4. Hanging Baskets:

Hanging baskets are an excellent option for those with limited space or who want to add a visual dimension to their gardens. They are typically made of plastic or wire and are designed to suspend plants, allowing them to cascade down. When choosing hanging baskets, ensure they have a sufficient number of drainage holes and consider the weight restrictions to avoid damage to your plants and the supporting structure.

## 5. Window Boxes:

Window boxes serve as a fantastic way to display plants and add charm to windows, balconies, or railings. They are usually made of wood, plastic, or metal. When selecting window boxes, pay attention to the material's durability and make sure they have adequate drainage holes to prevent water accumulation.

**Selecting the Right Soil Mixes:**

Equally important to selecting the right containers is choosing the appropriate soil mix for your plants. Here are some considerations when it comes to soil mixes:

**1. Potting Soil:**
Potting soil is a versatile mix that suits many plants' needs. It typically contains peat moss, perlite, vermiculite, and organic matter, providing a well-draining and nutrient-rich environment for plants. When choosing potting soil, opt for a high-quality organic blend that is specifically formulated for the types of plants you intend to grow.

**2. Garden Soil:**
Garden soil, also known as topsoil, is usually sourced directly from your garden and can be heavy and dense. It may contain clay, sand, or silt, and may require amendments to improve drainage and nutrient content. Garden soil should be sterilized to eliminate potential pests and diseases before using it in containers.

**3. Coir-based Mixes:**
Coir-based mixes are becoming increasingly popular due to their sustainable nature. Coir is derived from the fibrous outer husk of

coconuts and is a renewable resource. Coir-based mixes offer excellent water retention and drainage capabilities, and are an ideal choice for tropical or moisture-loving plants.

## 4. Cactus/Succulent Mix:

Cactus and succulent plants require well-draining soil mixes that mimic their natural habitats. Cactus/succulent mixes generally comprise a combination of regular potting soil, sand, and perlite to create the desired porous, fast-draining environment.

## 5. Specialty Blends:

Certain plants, such as orchids, require specific soil mixes tailored to their unique needs. There is a wide range of specialty blends available for various plant species, including orchids, African violets, and bonsai trees. These blends often incorporate specific ingredients, such as bark chips, sphagnum moss, or volcanic rock, to mimic the plants' natural environments and ensure optimal growth.

Selecting the right containers and soil mixes is crucial for successful gardening outcomes. By understanding the different types of containers and their pros and cons, you can provide an appropriate environment for your plants to thrive. Likewise, choosing the right soil mix ensures essential nutrients, proper water drainage, and appropriate aeration. We hope this chapter has provided you with valuable insights and practical recommendations to enhance your gardening journey. Remember, with the right containers and soil mixes, your plants will flourish, rewarding you with their beauty and vitality.

# Managing Space in Urban Settings

The rapid growth of urban populations has exerted tremendous pressure on available space in cities. As more people migrate from rural areas to urban centers in search of better opportunities, managing space in urban settings has become a critical challenge for city planners and policymakers. In this chapter, we will delve into various aspects of space management, including land-use planning, smart growth strategies, and sustainable development practices. By exploring these topics, we hope to shed light on the importance of managing space in urban settings and the potential solutions that can lead to more livable and vibrant cities.

## 9.3.1 Land-Use Planning:

One of the primary tools for managing space in urban settings is land-use planning. This practice involves determining the most appropriate use of land, such as residential, commercial, or industrial, to meet the needs of the growing population while optimizing available space. Land-use planning requires careful analysis of various factors, including demographics, economic trends, transportation infrastructure, and the protection of natural resources.

A crucial aspect of effective land-use planning is zoning, where the city is divided into different zones, each with specific regulations regarding land use, building height, and density. Zoning ensures that land is used efficiently and enables the coexistence of different activities within the city. For example, residential areas may be grouped separately from industrial zones to prevent pollution and reduce noise disturbances.

**9.3.2 Mixed-Use Development:**

Mixed-use development is another approach to managing space in urban settings. Instead of segregating different land uses, mixed-use development combines residential, commercial, and recreational spaces within the same area. This strategy encourages walkability, reduces vehicle dependence, and creates vibrant neighborhoods where people can live, work, and play.

By concentrating activities within a compact area, mixed-use development maximizes the efficiency of urban spaces and reduces the need for extensive transportation networks. Furthermore, this approach promotes social interaction and fosters a sense of community, ultimately enhancing the quality of life for residents.

**9.3.3 Smart Growth Strategies:**

To address the challenges of managing space in urban settings, many cities are adopting smart growth strategies. Smart growth emphasizes compact, transit-oriented, and sustainable development practices. It encourages the creation of walkable neighborhoods with mixed land uses, reducing the dependence on private vehicles and promoting public transportation options.

Through smart growth, cities strive to create communities where amenities are easily accessible, reducing the need for long commutes. This approach reduces congestion, lowers carbon emissions, and helps preserve natural areas by minimizing sprawl. Smart growth strategies also emphasize the preservation of historic and cultural landmarks to maintain the unique character of urban spaces.

### 9.3.4 Sustainable Development Practices:

Amidst growing concerns about climate change and environmental degradation, sustainable development practices have gained significant prominence in managing space in urban settings. Sustainable development seeks to strike a balance between economic growth, social well-being, and environmental conservation. It focuses on reducing energy consumption, promoting renewable energy sources, and enhancing resource efficiency.

Sustainable development also emphasizes green infrastructure, which includes the creation of parks, green spaces, and urban forests. These elements not only enhance the aesthetics of cities but also provide numerous benefits, such as improved air quality, temperature regulation, and stormwater management. Additionally, sustainable development practices prioritize the use of sustainable building materials and designs that reduce the environmental footprint of urban spaces.

### 9.3.5 Public Participation:

Effective management of space in urban settings requires the involvement of all stakeholders, particularly the public. Engaging citizens in the decision-making process for land-use planning, zoning regulations, and other development initiatives ensures that the space is used in a way that caters to their needs and aspirations.

Public participation can be facilitated through community gatherings, public hearings, and online platforms that encourage dialogue between citizens and policymakers. By incorporating diverse perspectives, cities can make more informed decisions that align with the collective vision for a sustainable and inclusive urban environment.

### 9.3.6 Addressing Inequality:

While managing space in urban settings is crucial, it is equally important to ensure that these efforts promote equitable access to resources and opportunities. Many cities face issues of social and economic inequality, where vulnerable communities are disproportionately affected by limited access to affordable housing, public amenities, and green spaces.

To address these disparities, urban planners need to actively consider and implement strategies that ensure equitable distribution of resources and opportunities. This includes the provision of affordable housing options, improving public transportation networks in underserved areas, and designing inclusive public spaces that cater to the needs of all residents, including children, the elderly, and people with disabilities.

Managing space in urban settings is an ongoing challenge that requires careful planning, innovative strategies, and participatory approaches. By adopting land-use planning, mixed-use development, smart growth strategies, and sustainable development practices, cities can optimize available space, create vibrant communities, and enhance residents' quality of life.

However, to achieve success, it is essential to prioritize inclusivity and equity throughout the planning process. By actively involving the public and addressing social and economic inequalities, cities can ensure that the benefits of managing space in urban settings are shared by all residents, fostering a more just and sustainable urban future.

# Vertical Gardening and Creative Solutions

In recent years, vertical gardening has emerged as a revolutionary concept in the field of horticulture. This innovative technique not only maximizes limited gardening spaces but also introduces an element of creativity and aesthetics into plant cultivation. Vertical gardens have gained popularity among urban dwellers, gardening enthusiasts, and architects alike, transforming blank walls, rooftops, and balconies into vibrant greenery. This chapter unravels the intricacies of vertical gardening, explores its benefits, and delves into the realm of creative solutions to enhance the visual appeal and functionality of these vertical landscapes.

**The Essence of Vertical Gardening:**

Vertical gardening is a concept that leverages the vertical plane to grow plants, utilizing structures such as trellises, containers, or modular systems. Unlike traditional gardening, which is mostly limited to horizontal spaces, vertical gardens offer a three-dimensional aspect, allowing plants to grow both upwards and outwards. This unique design not only makes efficient use of available space but also adds an element of architectural beauty to the surroundings.

**Benefits of Vertical Gardens:**

1. Space Optimization: One of the most significant advantages of vertical gardening is the efficient utilization of limited space. By growing plants vertically, one can maximize their gardening area, making it a perfect solution for small courtyards, balconies, or even indoor spaces.

2. Improved Air Quality: Vertical gardens act as natural air purifiers, absorbing carbon dioxide and emitting oxygen. These green walls help reduce air pollution, making them an ideal addition to urban environments where fresh air is a rare commodity.

3. Noise Reduction: Vertical gardens have proven to be effective in reducing noise levels, acting as a natural sound barrier. By absorbing sound waves, these living walls help create a more peaceful and serene atmosphere, especially in bustling city environments.

4. Temperature Regulation: Vertical gardens offer additional insulation, keeping the surrounding area cooler during summer and warmer during winter. This thermal regulation effect not only enhances comfort but also helps reduce energy consumption for indoor spaces.

5. Aesthetically Pleasing: Vertical gardens are a treat for the eyes, transforming dull walls into lush green landscapes. Their vibrant colors and textures bring a sense of serenity and beauty into any environment, enhancing the overall ambiance and aesthetics of the

surroundings.

**Creative Solutions in Vertical Gardening:**

**1. Modular Vertical Garden Systems:**

Modular systems, such as pocket gardens or living walls made from individual plant containers, have gained popularity due to their versatility and ease of maintenance. These systems allow for easy rearrangement, ensuring flexibility in plant choices and growth patterns. One can easily experiment with different plant combinations, adapting to changing seasons or personal preferences.

**2. Hydroponics and Aeroponics:**

Hydroponics and aeroponics are soil-less gardening techniques that work exceptionally well in vertical gardens. These systems provide a controlled environment for plants to grow efficiently, eliminating the need for traditional soil-based cultivation. By nourishing plants directly with nutrient-rich water, hydroponics and aeroponics simplify the growing process and minimize water usage.

**3. Green Roof Gardens:**
Green roofs are an innovative application of vertical gardening, turning otherwise unused rooftop spaces into vibrant gardens. These gardens not only provide insulation and temperature regulation benefits but also create pleasant outdoor spaces for relaxation and recreation. Green roofs are also known for their stormwater

management capabilities, reducing the load on urban drainage systems and minimizing the risk of flooding.

## 4. Moss Walls:

Moss wall installations have gained popularity for their unique aesthetic appeal and low maintenance requirements. Mosses are resilient, adaptable, and can thrive in low-light conditions, making them perfect choices for indoor vertical gardening. These living art pieces serve as beautiful focal points within homes, offices, or any space where a touch of nature is needed.

## 5. Vertical Herb and Vegetable Gardens:

Vertical gardening also offers an excellent opportunity for growing herbs and vegetables in limited spaces. By utilizing wall-mounted planters or trellises, one can create functional and productive gardens, providing a fresh supply of culinary delights. These gardens not only offer the convenience of having fresh herbs or vegetables readily available but also add a touch of greenery to kitchens and dining areas.

Vertical gardening has revolutionized the way we perceive and utilize space for plant cultivation. By extending gardening to the vertical plane, we can transform mundane walls into stunning green landscapes that offer numerous benefits. Whether it is optimizing limited space, improving air quality, or enhancing aesthetic appeal, vertical gardens provide creative solutions for every gardening enthusiast. The chapter has explored various techniques and applications, highlighting the immense potential of this unique horticultural concept.

# Chapter 9: Sharing the Harvest: Community Gardens and Beyond

Community gardens have been a part of human civilization for centuries, providing not only a source of fresh produce but also fostering a sense of community and shared responsibility. In this chapter, we delve into the world of community gardens and explore how they have evolved over time to become more than just spaces for growing food. We will discuss their benefits, challenges, and the potential they hold for building sustainable and resilient communities.

**The Historical Roots of Community Gardens**

To understand the significance of community gardens in today's society, it is important to look back at their historical roots. The concept of shared gardening dates back to ancient civilizations such as the Aztecs, who embraced chinampas or floating gardens to grow crops. Similarly, ancient Egyptians created rooftop gardens to combat limited arable land. These early examples highlight the ingenuity and resourcefulness of communities in finding ways to grow food collectively.

Fast forward to the 19th century, when urbanization and the

industrial revolution led to the emergence of community gardens in Europe and North America. These gardens provided a respite for city dwellers from the concrete jungle and allowed them to reconnect with nature. However, it was during World War I and II that community gardens truly gained momentum. With food shortages prevalent, these gardens became crucial in supplementing rationed supplies and fostering a sense of national unity.

**The Rise of Community Gardens in the Modern Era**

In recent years, community gardens have experienced a resurgence, driven by a confluence of factors such as growing concerns about food security, environmental sustainability, and the desire for social connectedness. Today, community gardens are not limited to urban settings but can be found in rural areas, schools, prisons, and even corporate campuses.

**Benefits of Community Gardens**

The benefits of community gardens extend far beyond the production of fresh, organic food. By bringing people together from diverse backgrounds, these gardens promote social cohesion and create opportunities for meaningful interactions. They serve as hubs for education and skill-sharing, where seasoned gardeners can mentor novices, and children can learn about the natural world. Community gardens also serve as habitats for diverse flora and fauna, supporting biodiversity in urban landscapes.

Moreover, community gardens offer therapeutic benefits, acting as spaces for stress relief and promoting mental well-being. Spending time in nature has been proven to reduce anxiety, improve mood, and enhance overall health. In addition, community gardens also contribute to the mitigation of climate change by reducing carbon emissions associated with long-distance transportation of food and sequestering carbon through plant growth.

**Challenges and Solutions**

While community gardens are undeniably beneficial, they do face several challenges that must be addressed for their continued success. One such challenge is limited access to suitable land, especially in urban areas where space is at a premium. Municipalities and governments must work together to identify vacant lots or underutilized spaces that can be converted into community gardens. Additionally, funding and resources are often limited, making it crucial for communities to come together and seek partnerships with local businesses, non-profit organizations, or government agencies to provide support for infrastructure and supplies.

Another challenge is ensuring long-term sustainability and the equitable distribution of garden resources. To tackle this, garden organizers need to implement fair distribution systems for plots, offer educational programs, and actively involve marginalized communities. It is also essential to create mechanisms for preserving and passing on gardening knowledge from one generation to the next.

**Beyond the Garden: Community Gardens as Catalysts for Change**

Community gardens have the potential to serve as catalysts for larger social and environmental transformations. They can become platforms for advocating for change, be it in local food policies, sustainability practices, or urban planning. Community leaders can use their collective power to raise awareness about issues such as food justice, environmental degradation, and the importance of green spaces in urban environments.

Furthermore, community gardens can foster economic resilience by providing opportunities for entrepreneurship, such as selling surplus produce at local markets or starting value-added food businesses. By supporting local economies and reducing dependence on global food systems, community gardens contribute to the creation of more resilient communities.

Chapter 10 has explored the rich history, benefits, challenges, and transformative potential of community gardens. From their ancient origins to their modern-day renaissance, community gardens have proven to be powerful tools for nourishing both the body and soul. As we move forward, it is essential to harness this potential and work towards creating more inclusive and sustainable communities that value the communal act of sharing the harvest.

# The Benefits of Community Gardening

Community gardening has emerged as a powerful and transformative movement with far-reaching benefits for both individuals and society as a whole. This chapter explores the manifold advantages of community gardening, from promoting physical and mental health to fostering social cohesion and environmental sustainability. Through an in-depth examination of various aspects and dimensions of community gardening, we aim to shed light on the profound impact this practice has on communities and the people who participate in it.

## 1. Improving Physical Health:

Many studies have highlighted the substantial physical health benefits associated with community gardening. Engaging in gardening activities offers a wide range of physical exercise, including digging, weeding, planting, and harvesting. These activities help individuals burn calories, enhance muscle strength, and improve cardiovascular health. Regular gardening also encourages individuals to spend more time outdoors, increasing their exposure to vitamin D, which is crucial for maintaining healthy bones and immune function.

Furthermore, the consumption of fresh, organic produce grown in community gardens promotes a healthier diet. Research has shown that individuals who participate in community gardening have higher intakes of fruits and vegetables, resulting in better nutrition and reduced risk of chronic diseases. Community gardens provide an accessible and affordable pathway for individuals to access nutrient-rich food, particularly in areas with limited food options.

**2. Enhancing Mental Well-being:**

Beyond its physical benefits, community gardening significantly impacts mental health and well-being. Immersion in nature has been proven to reduce stress, anxiety, and depression. The act of gardening itself fosters a sense of mindfulness, allowing individuals to be fully present in the moment and find solace in the therapeutic aspects of working with soil and plants.

Additionally, community gardens serve as spaces for social interaction and human connection, combating feelings of loneliness and isolation. Working collaboratively towards a shared goal, gardeners often form strong bonds and support networks, creating a sense of belonging and community spirit. The act of nurturing plants and observing their growth instills a sense of purpose and achievement, boosting self-esteem and providing a source of personal fulfillment.

**3. Promoting Environmental Sustainability:**

Community gardening plays a critical role in promoting environmental sustainability by fostering sustainable land use practices, reducing food waste, and encouraging biodiversity. Reclaiming unused land for the purpose of gardening helps combat urban sprawl and the loss of green spaces while increasing the overall utilization of available land resources.

Moreover, community gardens often prioritize organic and sustainable farming practices, avoiding the use of harmful chemicals and pesticides. By doing so, they promote the health and well-being of both humans and the natural environment. These gardens also act as important sanctuaries for pollinators, contributing to the conservation of essential insect populations and promoting the balance of ecosystems.

**4. Education and Skill Development:**
Community gardening provides valuable opportunities for educational and skill development, particularly for children and young adults. By involving young people in gardening activities, they learn about the natural world, horticulture, and environmental stewardship. This hands-on learning experience teaches important life skills, such as patience, responsibility, and teamwork.

Furthermore, community gardens often organize workshops and training sessions to share knowledge and expertise among participants. As gardeners learn from one another, they gain practical skills in gardening, plant propagation, composting, and soil management. Through these educational initiatives, community gardens contribute to the overall empowerment and self-sufficiency of individuals and communities.

**5. Food Security and Access:**
Community gardening plays a vital role in addressing food security

and access issues, particularly in underserved communities. By providing local, fresh produce, community gardens reduce reliance on long-distance food transportation, thus minimizing greenhouse gas emissions and combating climate change.

Furthermore, community gardens can help combat food deserts, which are areas where access to affordable, nutritious food is limited. Particularly in low-income urban neighborhoods, community gardens act as sources of affordable fresh produce, empowering community members to take control of their food choices and overall health.

Community gardening is a multifaceted practice that brings together physical health, mental well-being, social cohesion, environmental sustainability, and food security. Its benefits extend not only to individuals who engage directly with the gardens but also to the wider community and the environment. With its capacity to nurture physical and mental health, foster social connections, enhance environmental stewardship, and promote educational opportunities, community gardening has the potential to revolutionize the way we think about our food systems, public spaces, and overall well-being.

# Collaborative Garden Design and Management

In today's world, where the pace of life has accelerated, and urban spaces have become crowded and disconnected from nature, the importance of gardens and green spaces cannot be overstated. Gardens have always been a place of solace and tranquility, providing an escape from the hustle and bustle of the outside world. However, the traditional concept of a garden, as a space designed and managed by a single individual, is being reimagined.

Collaborative garden design and management is an emerging concept that emphasizes community involvement and shared responsibility. This approach recognizes that individual efforts alone might not be enough to create sustainable and thriving gardens. Instead, it encourages people to come together, pool their resources, and work collectively towards a common goal: the creation and maintenance of beautiful, functional, and environmentally friendly gardens.

**The Advantages of Collaboration:**

Collaborative garden design and management brings numerous benefits, both for the individuals involved and the wider community. Firstly, it promotes a sense of shared ownership and responsibility. When people work together to design and maintain a garden, they are more likely to have a sense of pride and attachment to the space.

This shared investment fosters a stronger commitment to long-term care and ensures the garden's survival for future generations.

Secondly, collaboration allows for the pooling of resources, skills, and expertise. Every individual brings a unique set of skills to the table, whether it be horticultural knowledge, landscaping expertise, or organizational abilities. By harnessing these diverse skills, a collaborative garden project can tap into a wealth of creativity and innovation, leading to more successful and dynamic garden designs.

Additionally, collaborative garden projects can foster social connections and community cohesion. When people work side by side, they forge meaningful relationships and strengthen the social fabric of their neighborhoods. These shared experiences create a sense of belonging and unity, reducing social isolation and improving overall well-being. Furthermore, collaborative gardens often become community hubs, providing opportunities for educational workshops, social gatherings, and cultural exchanges.

**Designing Collaborative Gardens:**

Designing a collaborative garden requires careful planning and consideration. The process should involve all stakeholders from the outset, including community members, local authorities, and relevant professionals. Here are some key steps to guide the design process:

1. Identify the Objectives: Begin by clarifying the goals and objectives

of the collaborative garden project. What purpose will the garden serve? Will it primarily focus on providing a beautiful aesthetic space, growing food, preserving biodiversity, or a combination of these?

2. Assess the Site: Conduct a thorough site analysis to identify the site's strengths, weaknesses, opportunities, and constraints. Consider factors such as soil quality, sunlight exposure, water availability, and existing vegetation. Assessing these elements will help inform the garden design, plant selection, and maintenance plan.

3. Engage the Community: Collaborative garden projects thrive on community involvement. Organize community meetings, workshops, and surveys to gather input from residents. Encourage active participation in the decision-making process to ensure that the garden design reflects the wishes and needs of the community.

4. Incorporate Diverse Elements: To create a vibrant and sustainable garden, incorporate diverse elements that cater to different functions and interests. Consider including vegetable beds, herb gardens, flower beds, water features, seating areas, and spaces for communal activities. Incorporating various elements will attract a broader range of users, fostering inclusivity and ensuring the garden's versatility.

5. Ensure Accessibility: A successful collaborative garden should be accessible to all members of the community, regardless of age or

physical abilities. Plan pathways that are wide, even, and wheelchair-friendly. Install raised beds or vertical gardens for individuals with mobility challenges. Designate shaded areas for rest and relaxation.

**Managing Collaborative Gardens:**

The successful long-term management of a collaborative garden is as crucial as its design. A well-managed garden ensures that it remains healthy, visually appealing, and continues to provide benefits to the community. Consider the following aspects while managing a collaborative garden:

1. Establish Clear Guidelines: Collaborative gardens require clear and transparent guidelines to maintain order and ensure everyone's involvement and responsibilities. Establish guidelines regarding gardening practices, maintenance schedules, and resource sharing. Regularly communicate these guidelines with all members involved in the garden project.

2. Develop a Maintenance Plan: To keep the collaborative garden thriving, develop a maintenance plan that outlines specific tasks and responsibilities. Distribute these responsibilities among volunteers, ensuring that all essential tasks, such as watering, weeding, pruning, and pest control, are covered. Regular maintenance should be built into the plan to prevent the garden from becoming neglected.

3. Provide Gardening Workshops and Training: Collaborative gardens often attract people with varying levels of gardening

experience. To empower participants and enhance their horticultural skills, organize regular workshops and training sessions. These initiatives can cover topics such as organic gardening practices, composting, pest management, and plant propagation.

4. Encourage Environmental Sustainability: Collaborative gardens have the potential to be environmentally sustainable spaces. Encourage the use of organic gardening practices, such as composting, companion planting, and water conservation techniques. Minimize the use of synthetic chemicals and invest in renewable energy sources, such as solar-powered irrigation systems.

5. Foster Community Engagement: The success of a collaborative garden relies heavily on community engagement. Continuously encourage community members to actively participate in garden-related activities. Organize events, such as harvest festivals or garden parties, to celebrate the garden's achievements and foster a sense of community pride.

Collaborative garden design and management provides a promising alternative to traditional, individual-centered approaches. By tapping into the collective wisdom, skills, and passion of community members, these projects can transform barren spaces into thriving, sustainable gardens. Through collaboration, people not only create beautiful landscapes but also build stronger and more resilient communities. Collaborative gardens hold the potential to renew our connection with nature, inspire creativity, and promote well-being for generations to come.

# Organizing Garden Workshops and Events

Gardening is not only a delightful hobby but also a rewarding form of self-expression. It allows individuals to connect with nature, nurture plants, and create beautiful outdoor spaces. To foster this passion for gardening, organizing workshops and events is an excellent way to engage with fellow enthusiasts, share knowledge, and enhance gardening skills. In this chapter, we will explore the art of organizing garden workshops and events, providing you with valuable insights and practical tips to make your endeavor a success.

## 1. Identifying the Purpose and Theme:

Before diving into the planning process, it is essential to identify the purpose and theme of your garden workshop or event. Consider what you want to achieve—spreading awareness, teaching specific techniques, or promoting community engagement. Once you have a clear objective in mind, choose a theme that aligns with your goals. For example, you might focus on organic gardening, urban landscapes, or floral arrangement.

## 2. Establishing the Format:

The format of your workshop or event will depend on various factors, including the target audience, available resources, and time constraints. Some common formats include lectures, hands-on demonstrations, panel discussions, and interactive sessions. A combination of formats can also be used to provide a comprehensive experience.

## 3. Choosing a Suitable Venue:

Selecting an appropriate venue is crucial in ensuring the success of your garden workshop or event. Consider the number of attendees, accessibility, parking facilities, and the availability of amenities such as restrooms and refreshment areas. Explore local botanical gardens, community centers, or private gardens that may offer suitable spaces for your event. Engaging in partnerships with such venues can provide additional benefits, such as reduced costs or promotional support.

## 4. Booking Knowledgeable Speakers and Instructors:

The success of any garden workshop or event largely depends on the expertise and knowledge of the speakers and instructors involved. Identify individuals who are well-versed in the chosen theme and have the ability to engage and educate participants. Reach out to local horticulturalists, landscape designers, experienced gardeners, or even renowned authors who can add value with their insights. Ensure that the speakers' schedules align with the chosen date and time of the event.

**5. Creating a Well-Structured Agenda:**

To ensure a smooth flow of activities, it is essential to create a well-structured agenda for your garden workshop or event. Start by determining the length of your event and divide it into various time slots accordingly. Allocate sufficient time for each activity, including breaks, Q&A sessions, and networking opportunities. Make sure the activities are arranged in a logical sequence, creating a cohesive learning experience for participants.

**6. Promoting Your Workshop or Event:**

To attract attendees, effective promotion is paramount. Utilize diverse marketing channels, both online and offline, to reach a broad audience. Create visually appealing flyers or posters to distribute around gardening centers, community boards, and local businesses. Leverage social media platforms to create event pages, share engaging content, and collaborate with relevant gardening influencers. Additionally, consider reaching out to local newspapers, radio stations, or gardening magazines for event listings or press coverage.

**7. Arranging Required Materials and Supplies:**

To ensure a seamless workshop or event, make a comprehensive list of all the materials and supplies you will need. This may include seating arrangements, audio-visual equipment, projectors, microphones, signage, writing materials, and refreshments. Reach out to local businesses, gardening suppliers, or sponsors who may be willing to provide support or sponsor certain aspects of your event.

## 8. Implementing Practical Demonstrations and Hands-on Activities:

To maximize participant engagement and learning, integrate practical demonstrations and hands-on activities into your garden workshop or event. This provides attendees with the opportunity to directly apply newfound knowledge and skills. For example, you could include activities like potting plants, creating floral arrangements, or designing miniature landscapes. Ensure you have enough resources and supplies available for all participants, including plants, pots, tools, and materials.

## 9. Engaging Participants with Q&A Sessions and Panel Discussions:

Including question-and-answer sessions and panel discussions in your workshop or event encourages active participation and engagement. Allocate sufficient time after each session for participants to ask questions, seek clarifications, and share their experiences. Panel discussions can also be an excellent platform for experts to exchange ideas, offer diverse perspectives, and inspire attendees with their collective knowledge.

## 10. Providing Networking Opportunities:

Don't underestimate the importance of networking in garden workshops and events. Encourage participants to connect with one another, fostering a sense of community and enabling knowledge-sharing beyond the workshop or event. Allocate time for informal interactions, where participants can exchange contact information, socialize, and discuss gardening-related topics. Facilitate networking opportunities by organizing refreshment breaks, garden tours, or even small group activities.

Organizing garden workshops and events can be an enriching experience for both organizers and participants. The process requires meticulous planning, attention to detail, and a passion for gardening. By identifying the purpose and theme, establishing the format, choosing a suitable venue, booking knowledgeable speakers and instructors, creating a well-structured agenda, promoting the event effectively, arranging required materials and supplies, implementing practical activities, engaging participants through Q&A sessions and panel discussions, and providing networking opportunities, you can ensure the success of your garden workshop or event. May your efforts inspire and empower fellow gardening enthusiasts to cultivate their love for plants and create their own natural havens.